*Sa*

# *A Guide to walking the last 100km of the Camino Francés*

## M. J. McCarthy

# Table of Contents

# Chapter 1 - Is this book for you?

## Are you sort of interested in walking the Camino Francés but don't know much about it yet?

Well **yes**, then this book is for you. This guide will give you a straight forward introduction to walking the last 100km of the Camino. This book will take you through what it is likely to cost you both in terms of money and vacation days and how to minimise the cost. It will then lead you through how to prepare, what equipment is worth buying, what are the essentials to pack, what to leave at home and what you might consider bringing but is not essential. From the basics of packing the book will take you through where and how to start. The guide will lead you through the last 100km of the Camino, from village to village with maps of each village. These simple maps identify where the water fountains are, the cafés, the restaurants, the pharmacists and most importantly where the albergues (the pilgrim hostels) are located. I have put great effort into establishing accurate distances which includes the extra distance walked as you go up and the downhill. The distances given in this book are the most accurate available in any Camino guidebook. What initially motivated me to write this guidebook was frustration at the inaccurate distances and elevation charts in the current crop of guidebooks, which seemed to constantly under call both the distance and the steepness of ascents and descents. In addition, what further sets this guide apart from the other guides are the estimated walking times which accurately reflect the natural speed variations as you walk uphill and downhill. I give six time estimations for each distance village to village which reflect accurately how long it will take based on your natural walking pace. I believe that the Camino is a fantastic experience for all and that all includes the majority of us who God never designed to be athletes. This guide is designed to include detailed GPS coordinates of all accommodation to allow you at the end of a hard days walking to find your accommodation quickly and without stress. This guide provides details of cost, telephone number, GPS coordinates, address, email address and website (if available) for all albergues (pilgrim hostels). The guide will provide suggested daily itineraries (i.e. where to stop and stay) but I would ask that you try not to follow the suggested itineraries too closely as I strongly believe that in doing so you will miss out on making the Camino your own personal Camino. Also, some of the most interesting and welcoming albergues are to be found in the towns and villages in between the suggested stages. Try always to keep this one thought about the Camino in your mind and that is this *the Camino is not about the destination, it is not about arriving it is instead about The Way*. So, please take time and try and enjoy your Camino. At the beginning, it is hard not be sucked in to constantly moving quickly in a desire to get to Santiago but please try to resist and take as much time as you can spare to savour the experience.

## Have you walked the Camino before and are looking for an updated guidebook?

Again, **yes**, this guidebook is designed to give you accurate distances, maps which you don't need the internet available to look up and good estimates of how long it will take to walk to the next village. This guide will also provide you with detailed GPS coordinates not only for the next village but more usefully of every albergue on the route. So, when you arrive at your overnight stopping place you don't have to spend 10 minutes looking over the village map trying to work out where you are meant to be staying. In addition, this guide includes the latest cost, telephone number, email and web address (if available) for all pilgrim accommodation along the way. When experienced as an eBook on a smartphone, this guidebook provides automatic links to phone numbers, GPS coordinates and web addresses.

## You want recommendations for good or cheap places to stay?

**Yes** and **no**. Even in e-book it is difficult to keep an up to date set of recommendations. I have therefore kept recommendations for albergues out of this book. In general, I list the cheapest and biggest albergues first and the more expensive and smaller (and therefore generally better) albergues last. Also, if you want a list of recommended albergues please look at the Facebook page associated with this book:
www.facebook.com/SarriatoSantiago

## Are you planning to walk the whole of the Camino Francés?

Then no, while this guide will help you booking accommodation with last week of your Camino, you will need to purchase one of the many good guides with details of accommodation for the whole Camino.

## Why a special version for the last 100km?

That is because it is the most popular starting point and approximately a third of all pilgrims on the Camino Francés start their pilgrimage from Sarria. The reason why so many start from Sarria is that it is the last major starting point that allows a walking pilgrim to qualify for the official Compostela certificate. The fact that it only takes just under a week from Sarria makes it very attractive for those who are short of vacation. Starting in Sarria can be a great option for those who wish to arrive in Santiago for the feast of St James (which starts on the evening of July 24th and lasts till the evening of July 25th) but who are restricted on start date by other commitments such as exams. More on the Compostela and how to qualify for it later but suffice to say at this point the bishop of Santiago sets out minimum qualifying distance as being 100 km by foot or by horse and 200 km by bicycle.

## Why choose this guidebook as opposed to the other good guidebooks?

1. It is focused on the needs of the pilgrims starting in Sarria including sections on how to get to Sarria and where to get any last-minute equipment in Sarria.
2. This guidebook provides 3D distances which includes the extra distance incurred by walking uphill and downhill to provide the most accurate distances available in any guidebook.
3. This guidebook provides the most accurate elevation maps available for the Camino which allows you to gauge the difficulty of each stage and plan accordingly.
4. This guidebook provides the most accurate estimated walking time available which recognizes that the speed at which people walk is affected by going up and down slopes. It can be extremely discouraging to attempt to maintain 4km/hr going up a steep slope. I believe it helps to recognize that you need to adjust your walking pace to steepness of the slope.
5. This guidebook provides more village maps than any other guidebook currently available for this stretch of the Camino. The village maps are useful for finding albergues that are not directly on the Camino as well as other amenities such as convenience shops and drinking fountains.
6. This guidebook is very competitively priced against similar guidebooks. It also combines packing and planning advice avoiding the need to buy an additional specialised book.

7. The Kindle version of this guide is one of only two guidebooks that automatically links to important websites. Only this guidebook provides links to websites to every albergue that currently has a website and that is the majority of albergues.

8. If you are reading this on a smartphone or tablet or you have any other GPS enabled device, this is the only guidebook that provides GPS coordinates for every albergue.

9. The Kindle version of this guide provides clickable links to the email of each albergue that publishes their email address allowing you to email your booking or query.

## Which version is best for you paperback or Kindle?

I currently sell twice as many paperbacks as I do Kindle versions. Most pilgrims want the security and "user friendliness" of a proper paperback. The Kindle version with its direct links to websites, email addresses and phone numbers is great for advance planning of your Camino. However, when on Camino most pilgrims appear to prefer using the paperback for ease of access. Many pilgrims like to take notes in their paperback edition and to keep as it a memento of their Camino. Personally, I prefer the Kindle edition for the ease of making phone calls to book ahead but I am in the minority. If you purchase the paperback from Amazon.com, Amazon run a match book program whereby you can also buy the Kindle version for $1.99. Unfortunately match book is not yet available on any of the international Amazon sites yet.

# Chapter 2 - The Complete Guide to Your Backpack and other Planning

## When to walk?

The pilgrimage season from Sarria starts at Easter and lasts until the October school holidays. From November through March as few as 7 pilgrims a day set out from Sarria compared with the peak weeks in August when 500 pilgrims a day set off from Sarria. The largest number of pilgrims, however, set out from Sarria in the third week of July when pilgrim numbers on the Sarria leg swell to several thousand per day. This is because these pilgrims can arrive in Santiago for the evening of the Feast of St James (July 24th). This is a both a fantastic and terrible time to do your pilgrimage. Fantastic from the perspective of being able to celebrate the Feast of Saint James in Santiago, terrible from the fact that all albergues are fully booked and you will likely end up sleeping in one of the local schools which open up to absorb the huge numbers of additional pilgrims. Whichever week you choose to walk your Camino from Sarria to Santiago I hope you find the experience as moving and as fulfilling as I and so many others have and hope it gives you the taste to do one of the longer Caminos where you have so much more time to find peace, friendship and contentment on your Camino.

## Which footwear to buy?

This is a subject of constant debate on the various Camino Facebook pages and online forums. I will try and layout the various opinions in as a balanced fashion as I can so that you can make your own mind up and choose the right footwear for you.

What is agreed by everyone is that you need to walk in your footwear before you go on Camino. The consensus is that you need at least two weeks of wearing your footwear in lieu of normal shoes. During this period, I wouldn't go on any long practice walks but maybe a few short ones towards the end of the two weeks.

Time of the year will affect your choice as if you are walking anytime from November till April the route through Galicia can be very muddy which strongly favours the selection towards boots. In the summer, the heat pushes the choice more towards running shoes or walking sandals.

If you choose boots, then you must choose between leather or synthetic boots. The leather boots are tougher but are hotter and take several more weeks to walk in.

Please always select your footwear in a store where you can try on a wide variety of footwear. Remember if they feel right they are likely to be right. If walking in the heat of the summer your feet will expand slightly during the day, so you may need to go one European (half a US/UK) size above your normal size.

If you are in anyway unsure on your feet, then this would favour boots with ankle support. If you struggle with the heat, then this would favour the choice of walking sandals with toe protection. Having walked with a fellow pilgrim who made a 4500km Camino in the summer, he strongly advocated walking sandals.

Personally, I have tried boots, walking shoes and walking sandals and I now take a combination of synthetic boots and walking sandals for summer Caminos and synthetic boots and crocs for winter Caminos. In the summer, I often switch to walking sandals for the last 4 or 5km to let my feet cool down a little. I have walked a 900km Camino with walking shoes which was a good compromise for most of the Camino but was not great on rocky paths and descents, so I have switched back to more robust synthetic boots. My parting piece of advice is to choose the footwear that feels right for you!

## Which Backpack to buy?

Backpacks are like boots; you must at least try them on in a shop before buying them. Ordering them on the internet without having found out which feels most comfortable for you first is a false economy. If you are walking in the summer months you should be looking at a pack size of between 33 and 40 litres. Although some people can get by with a smaller pack size (even as small as 20 litres). These ultra-small packs not only make it very difficult to locate individual items but make it difficult every morning to repack your bag in a dark dorm room. Additionally, important features such as an offset mesh back and adjustable back length are not available on these ultra-small packs. When travelling from October till May it is advisable to bring a sleeping bag. Sleeping bags vary in packed size from about 7 litres to about 17 litres so you may need to be looking for a 40 to 55 litre pack for a winter Camino. There are plenty of good brands out on the market, so look to pay no more than about €100. After size and weight, one of the other important factors in your selection of a backpack is whether the backpack is height adjustable. An adjustable back height feature is important to get the majority of the weight resting on your hips. Especially for a summer Camino a backpack with an off-set mesh back that allows your back to breathe is highly desirable as you can lose significant amounts of water through you back and you may have to carry more water to compensate.

## How much should your pack weigh?

The rule of thumb is no more than 10% of your body weight and this is a very good rule of thumb. If you are an average woman this gives you 8kg (18lb) to play with of which about 1.5kg (3lb) will be taken up by your backpack. For young adults and those with smaller frames this rule gives you just 6kg (13lb) to play with. For those who do have little weight to play with, it may be worth going beyond €100 and investing in an ultra-light weight backpack from the likes of Deuter, Osprey or Lowe Alpine as this can give you up to another kilogram (2lb) to work with. Alternatively, it might be worth considering using one of the dedicated backpack transportation services.

## Should I carry or ship my pack?

There are some people who think to be a "true pilgrim" one must always carry one's own backpack. To me the concept of trying to be a "true pilgrim" misses the point of pilgrimage in that pilgrimage is something God does for us not something we do for God. Pilgrimage is a special time for us to reflect on life and be at one with the world, whether you carry your pack or not is not critical to this. Having said that, I personally normally choose to carry my own pack as I really enjoy the freedom it gives me especially on the longer 800km+ Caminos. On the Sarria to Santiago route if I am travelling with a group I usually encourage people to ship their pack and just carry a day pack. The reason I do this is that when travelling in a group it is advisable to pre-book accommodation in private albergues (municipal and parish albergues will generally not allow advance bookings) so you can keep the group together. Therefore, there is no need for flexibility. Additionally, for most people the first three days of pilgrimage are the physically the toughest and having your pack shipped can make an enormous difference. The cost of having your pack shipped on the Sarria to Santiago route is currently somewhere between 3 and 5 euros per day per bag or you can buy a package which costs from €20 for the whole trip.

# How do I ship my pack?

There are a number of companies that ship packs on the Sarria to Santiago route. The feedback on all these companies is generally very good. The process is that you get labels to stick on each bag with your name, the name and the town of the albergue you are shipping from and most importantly the albergue and town you are shipping to. You will also get an envelope to put the money inside which you tie to the bag. If you are in a group and shipping more than one pack you only have to have prepare one envelope to cover all the bags, but each bag must have its own label. The evening before you must call the transportation company (don't worry if you don't speak any Spanish as they speak and understand basic English) to tell them that there are bags to collect from your albergue and where they are to be shipped to. The albergues have little or no control over the shipping companies so sometimes they are reluctant to get too involved in the process of shipping bags other than to provide the labels and an area in the reception to leave the bags to be shipped. However, some of the better albergues will provide a range of labels from different shipping companies to give you a choice, they will also help with change for the envelope and some will even make the phone call to the transportation company for you. You do not have to stay in the albergue where you are having the bag shipped to. Some people have their packs shipped to one of the central albergues and then look around at a couple of albergues before deciding where to stay at. But obviously if you know where you are staying it is better to get your bags shipped directly there. There is generally a weight limit of 15kg on the packs but from personal observation the shipping companies seem not to enforce this rule. Some people take a dedicated bag between two people to save money.

There are a number of companies that ship packs on the Sarria to Santiago route. The feedback on all these companies is generally very good:

- CAMINO COMODO (caminocomodo.es) Telephone: +34 6 1775 4440Email: caminocomodogalicia@gmail.com
- MOCHILAS DAVID (mochilasdavid.es) Telephone: +34 6 5908 4551Email: reservas@mochilasdavid.es
- PILBEO.COM (www.pilbeo.com) Telephone: +34 6 7064 8078Email: contact@pilbeo.com
- CAMINOFÁCIL (caminofacil.net/en/) Telephone: +34 6 1079 8138Email: contacto@caminofacil.net

- CORREOS(Spanish Postal Service) (www.elcaminoconcorreos.com/es/transporte-mochilas.php) Telephone: **+34 6 0661 8341**Email: **mimochila@correos.com**
- JACOTRANS(www.jacotrans.com) Telephone: **+34 6 0604 9858**Email: **jacotrans@gmail.com**

Some of these companies offer a package rate for the whole journey. Currently the most competitive of these is the Spanish postal service (Correos) which offers a flat fee of €20 to ship your bag each day from Sarria to Santiago irrespective of how many days you take.

# What Not to Pack?

I have put this section first as it is more helpful to tell you what you don't need rather than what you do need.

- Tent. Why? They are just too heavy (starting at about 3kg/6lb) and you will not save money by camping. Most large albergues cost €6 to €10 a night and offer kitchen facilities so you can prepare your own food. Being able to prepare your own food will save you the majority of the €6 to €10 as food and refreshments will outweigh your accommodation cost by a factor of at least 2:1. A few of the hostels are donativo in which case you just pay what you can afford even if that is nothing and with this they often offer a donativo evening meal.
- Stove. As above, many albergues have kitchen facilities. Further, a stove with fuel is both heavy and a fire risk and one which you will not be permitted to use where there is any risk of forest fires.
- Sleeping bag. Well at least in the summer months, a sleeping bag liner together with extra clothes should be sufficient. Most but not all albergues will provide blankets if you ask. In the winter months, a sleeping bag is a must. To minimise the weight, it is worth investing in a superlite (about 850g/30oz) sleeping bag which can be obtained for about €60 but it's probably not worth spending €200 on the ultralite (about 650g/23oz) sleeping bags.
- Cutlery. Anything made of steel even small items are heavy. If you are preparing your own food in an Albergue there will be cutlery there for you to use and if you are eating in a bar or restaurant they will provide cutlery. Some people bring a polycarbonate spork with them so they can enjoy a yoghurt or make their own sandwich at lunch time but most pilgrims

don't even bother with a spork. A spork is a combined spoon, fork and knife. They come in steel, aluminium and polycarbonate but the polycarbonate version is the lightest and therefore the best.

- Sat Nav system. Take a smartphone or tablet with GPS capability instead but make sure you download the apps and most importantly the maps for Spain before you set off as these are often huge.
- Toiletries. Don't take any full size toiletries, stick with the 100ml limit set by the airlines and buy replacement toiletries if you run out. The extra cost of buying these in small quantities from convenience stores along the way is a price well worth paying to avoid the extra weight of full sized containers.
- Separate shampoo and body wash. Buy a simple shampoo that you can use as body wash as well.
- Razor blades. Just buy, use and dispose of disposable razor blades from the local stores as and when you need them.
- Non-walking clothes. If you want some smart clothes for a few days stay in Santiago, you have a couple of choices. If you pass through Santiago on your way to Sarria you can leave a bag with all your smart clothes at Casa Ivar (www.casaivar.com/luggage-storage-in-santiago-de-compostela/index.html). Alternatively, you can post ahead some smart clothes to yourself for collection at the Santiago Post Office or at Casa Ivar. Thirdly and perhaps most simply use one of the luggage transfer services. Only carry what you are going to use each day.
- Spare shoes. Shoes are very heavy. You will need something for your feet as most albergue will ask you to leave your boots or walking shoes outside but something very light such as crocs should be your only alternative footwear.
- A compass. The Camino is marked by yellow arrows along the entire route. It is entirely possible to walk the whole Camino without a guide nor a map nor a compass. Though as a guidebook writer I am hoping you will obviously see the advantages of using a guidebook. If you still feel the need for a compass remember there are many good compass apps you can download to your smartphone.
- A camera. Modern smartphones provide superb quality photographs as well as high quality videos. There are numerous advantages of using your phone for taking photographs including ease of uploading and always being to hand but the most important reason is to save weight.

- Cotton clothes. Cotton is a relatively heavy fabric when compared to modern synthetic material. It holds moisture against your skin rather than taking it away from your skin. The only two natural fibres you should consider using are silk and merino wool. Otherwise all your clothing should be fully synthetic. The main reason for this is weight but also synthetic materials are easier to clean and dry.
- A pillow. Virtually all albergues will provide a pillow. If no pillows are available just use some of your clothes.
- Makeup. Most people who carry makeup, end up not using it during the Camino, as they are just too physically tired to invest the time in putting on makeup. If you want some for the end of your Camino, do as I have suggested for smart clothes. i.e. send ahead to Santiago or more simply use one of the baggage transfer services.

## What you should definitely pack?

- A Smartphone. These are versatile and useful and everyone has one, so they are not the target for thieves they once were. Your smartphone will act as your watch, your alarm clock, your camera, your guidebook, your email and internet connection as well as your phone.
- A very good charger i.e. a charger that can charge at least 2000mA. If you carry more than one device that will need charging, then buy a charger which charge both at the same time. Charging points are still scarce in most albergues so it's important not to hog a charging point with a charger that takes 8 hours to recharge your phone. While you may not be making phone calls every day, remember your phone is also your camera and you will want to keep it with enough charge to take photographs along the way. If you are struggling with battery charge, airplane mode saves battery but allows you to use GPS and take photographs.
- One fleece. Even in the summer, there will be times you will need to keep warm.
- Sun Cream with a minimum of factor 15. You need to make sure you get into the habit of reapplying the sun cream at the end of every break and despite it's cost you will need to purchase more along the way and use even if you have developed a sun tan.

- Deodorant. Keep the amount of deodorant you carry to a bare minimum again no more than 100ml and buy replacement deodorant along the way.
- Water containers to carry at least 2 litres of fluid.
- 3 pairs of underwear.
- 3 pairs of walking socks, preferably made from merino wool as merino wool kills off the bacteria which causes foot odour.
- 3 wicking (walking type) t-shirts. Most modern walking and running type t-shirts are designed so the fibres act as wicks which draw moisture away from your skin keeping your skin dry which is important on long strenuous walks.
- 2 pairs of walking trousers, preferably ones which can be converted to shorts and 1 pair of shorts or 2 pairs of shorts and 1 pair of trousers. Trousers are essential if the weather is poor or if you are vulnerable to sunburn.
- A large microfibre bath towel.
- Paper tissues or toilet roll, if you need to go to the toilet in the great outdoors.
- Wet wipes to clean your hands afterwards.
- Small plastic bags (poop bag style). To carry your used paper tissues, wet wipes or any other rubbish with you until you reach a bin.
- A poncho or lightweight raincoat with good waterproofing characteristics. The rain in Spain does not mainly fall on the plains; it mainly falls on Galicia! There is a reason why Galicia is beautifully green and lush so assume even it peak summer that it will rain heavily on at least one day.
- A raincover for your backpack. Most good backpacks will have an integrated raincover at the very top or very bottom of your backpack which you just pull out.
- A sun hat.
- A pumice stone to rub off dead skin and keep your feet supple.
- Ear plugs. You will be sleeping in dormitories. Many people snore when they sleep. Some snore very loudly. It is therefore worth investing in good ear plugs. In terms of determining how good ear plugs are, you need to look for SNR number in Europe and the NRR number in North America. There are only very slight differences between these two rating systems and the higher the rating the better. You should be looking to buy plugs with a rating of 33 or above. Some suitable ear plugs are: the 3M E-A-Rsoft FX Earplugs, the Howard Leight MAX and the HEAROS Xtreme Protection.

- 7mm PodoPro felt pad (available via Ebay). You can stick this to your foot with a cut out for the blister so you can walk without putting any pressure on the blister itself. This will get you through the first 24 hours of a blister, after which time the blister can be drained. These are in lieu of Compeed plasters which cannot be shaped to your specific blister. You will need scissors to cut the felt pad but I would borrow scissors from where I was staying rather than carry the additional weight.

# Non-essentials you might want to pack?

- A Kindle in place of any paper books as a Kindle weighs less than even just one book and one charge will last your whole Camino. A Kindle with 3G capability can be used as a simple web browser without incurring any additional roaming charges or needing wifi
- Extra underwear.
- A long sleeve wicking type walking t-shirt. You can always layer up with multiple t-shirts if you feel the cold at night.
- Walking sticks/poles. Most pilgrims use either walking sticks or a wooden staff, some even use a branch they find along the way. They are particularly helpful when going around muddy patches, going uphill and even more so going downhill. Research shows that you burn more energy when using walking sticks but advocates point out that it takes strain of your legs and feet. The stretch from Sarria to Santiago is very hilly but doesn't have the very steep descents that mandate the use of walking poles. In Winter and Spring, the paths particularly from Palas de Rei to Arzua can be very muddy and even partially flooded. This is where a pole or a stick is probably essential. In summer and early autumn, I have walked without poles, mainly to avoid the extortionate hold luggage fees (as most airlines and some countries including the UK explicitly prohibit carrying walking poles in cabin luggage). It is ultimately a question of personal taste as to whether you use walking sticks or not but the consensus appears to be moving towards most people favouring the use of walking poles. If you do choose to use walking poles it is recommended to spend some time learning on how to use the poles effectively. There are some excellent YouTube videos which will help you get the most benefit from your walking sticks. When it comes to walking sticks the consensus is that

anti-shock mechanisms add unnecessary weight to walking sticks and any benefits gained from going downhill with anti-shock are outweighed by the extra effort in going uphill with anti-shock. For cushioning, the better quality sticks come with cork handles or similar. The better poles also come with quick lock rather than twist tightening. In terms of weight there is a premium for lightweight with carbon fibre poles being the most expensive (expect to pay €70 upwards). Due to the extortionate cost of hold luggage, some people who travel with packs small enough to fit into cabin luggage (including my wife and myself) are now buying cheap walking poles (about €12 each pole) from Peregrinoteca in Sarria and then just ditching them in Santiago.

- A micro-down ultra-light jacket (not required in the summer). This can double up as a very good pillow.
- A guidebook. Despite having a financial interest in encouraging you to purchase a guidebook, the reality is that you simply do not need a guidebook. You can simply follow the yellow arrows (flechas amarillas) all the way from Sarria without ever referring to a guidebook. Additionally, fellow pilgrims will generally let you consult their guidebook if you need to. Having said all that, a guidebook does make life easier. It helps you decide how far you want to walk each day. It helps you during the day in deciding whether to call it a day or to push on to the next village. It helps you decide which albergue you can afford and which albergue you are likely to prefer. It lets you phone or email ahead and ensure you have somewhere to sleep that night. It gives you background to where you are and it helps you plan the challenge ahead, knowing how steep and how long the hike to the next stop will take. Generally, it is a good idea to have your own guidebook with you and I hope you choose this guidebook.
- A small LED torch. You can use your smartphone at night around the albergue but if you are doing any early morning walking, then a head torch is worth the extra weight required.
- Waterproof trousers. They are light and are probably worth packing but are not essential.
- A coarse mesh laundry bag to put your dirty washing in. This also facilitates sharing washing machines and tumble dryers with other pilgrims.

# How to get to Sarria

- By train from Madrid there are three daytime services and an overnight sleeper service (with the exception of Saturday night) from Madrid Charmartin. The cost of your ticket to Sarria will cover getting the train from Madrid Airport to Charmatin. But to be honest I usually cheat and get a taxi which has a flat fee of €30 and takes 20 minutes. The cost of the tickets from Madrid to Sarria is about 30 euro for the daytime services and 80 euro for the overnight sleeper.
- By train from Barcelona there are two daytime services from Barcelona Sants and an overnight service. The overnight service costs about 100 euro for a recliner seat and about 200 euro for a bed. The daytime services cost from 50 euro, take up to 11 and half hours and pick up from Pamplona, Zaragoza, Burgos and Leon among other sites.
- For further details on train services in Spain contact Renfe (www.renfe.com +34 9 0232 0320).

## Train timetable from Madrid

| MADRID CHARMARTIN | SARRIA |
|---|---|
| 07:15 | 13:14 |
| 13:05 | 18:59 |
| 15:00 | 21:07 |
| 22:14 | 06:42 |

## Train timetable from Barcelona

| BARCELONA SANTS | SARRIA |
|---|---|
| 09:00 | 18:59 |
| 09:30 | 21:07 |
| 20:20 | 09:01 |

- By coach from Santiago. It may sound strange to fly to Santiago to get the bus to Sarria and then to walk back to Santiago. However, this is one of the most popular routes to get to Sarria and makes the return journey home easier. There are no direct buses from Santiago to Sarria. However, the Empresa Freire bus to Lugo stops directly outside Santiago airport terminal. If you choose to visit Santiago first, then you can get the same bus from Santiago main bus station. The bus to Lugo takes about two hours and cost about 10 euro. You must then go inside Lugo bus terminal and go to the Monbus desk and buy the ticket to Sarria which costs about €4. Unfortunately, you cannot buy a combined ticket to Sarria so you need to buy the ticket for the journey to Lugo as you board the bus at Santiago airport and then the separate ticket for Sarria in Lugo bus station. For further details, contact La Empresa Freire (www.empresafreire.com) and Monbus (www.monbus.es/en).

## Coach Timetable

As of June 2017 the current timetable is as follows:

### Mondays to Fridays

| SANTIAGO | AIRPORT | ARRIVE LUGO | DEPART LUGO | SARRIA |
|---|---|---|---|---|
| 07:00 | 07:10 | 09:00 | 10:35 | 11:10 |
| 09:15 | 09:25 | 11:25 | 12:00 | 12:35 |
| 11:00 | 11:10 | 12:35 | 12:45 | 13:20 |
| 12:45 | 12:55 | 14:45 | 15:20 | 15:55 |
| 14:40 | N/A | 16:40 | 17:30 | 18:01 |
| 16:00 | 16:10 | 18:05 | 18:35 | 19:10 |
| 17:00 | N/A | 18:35 | 20:00 | 20:35 |
| 18:30 | 18:40 | 20:30 | 20:45 | 21:15 |
| 20:00 | 20:10 | 21:55 | 22:00 | 22:35 |

## Saturdays

| SANTIAGO | AIRPORT | ARRIVE LUGO | DEPART LUGO | SARRIA |
|----------|---------|-------------|-------------|--------|
| 07:00 | 07:10 | 09:00 | 10:35 | 11:10 |
| 11:00 | 11:10 | 13:00 | 13:45 | 14:15 |
| 12:45 | 12:55 | 14:45 | 15:50 | 16:25 |
| 16:00 | 16:10 | 18:05 | 18:35 | 19:10 |
| 17:00 | N/A | 18:35 | 18:35 | 19:10 |
| 18:30 | 18:40 | 20:30 | 20:45 | 21:15 |

## Sundays

| SANTIAGO | AIRPORT | ARRIVE LUGO | DEPART LUGO | SARRIA |
|----------|---------|-------------|-------------|--------|
| 07:00 | 07:10 | 09:00 | 10:35 | 11:10 |
| 11:00 | 11:10 | 13:00 | 13:45 | 14:15 |
| 16:00 | 16:10 | 18:05 | 18:35 | 19:10 |
| 17:00 | N/A | 18:35 | 18:35 | 19:10 |
| 18:30 | 18:40 | 20:30 | 20:45 | 21:15 |
| 20:00 | N/A | 22:00 | 22:30 | 23:05 |

- By private hire direct from Santiago airport. This can be an expensive (about €130) option but if there are 3 or 4 of you this is affordable and gets you to Sarria and saves an additional overnight stay in Santiago. The journey takes about an hour and a half. There are several companies you can pre-book and it is definitely worth shopping around. Some of the many companies that offer pre-booking include:
    o Taxi Galicia.com (www.taxigalicia.com)
    o Xacotrans (www.xacotrans.com)
    o Galicia Incoming (www.galiciaincoming.com)
    o Taxi Peregrino.com (www.taxiperegrino.com)
    o Taxi Galicia.eu (www.Taxigalicia.eu)

      o   Taxi Peregrino.es (www.peregrinotaxi.es)
- By coach to Santiago from Oporto, Vigo and La Coruna via ALSA (www.alsa.es).

# How much will it cost?

- On a very tight budget you can live on €30 per day which roughly breaks down to €10 for accommodation, €10 for your evening meal, €6.50 for lunch and €3.50 for breakfast. However, this is a very tight budget and most pilgrims tend to budget on about €35-€40 a day as a much more realistic figure. Santiago is significantly more expensive than being on the Camino. You should budget for about €55 a day as a minimum for Santiago itself.

# How do you keep the cost down?

- Most of your money will be spent not on accommodation but on drinks and food and here just sticking to water which is free will save you significant amounts of money as well as being healthier. Most albergues also have a kitchen facility and this is by far the best way to save money, not only by preparing your own evening meal but also by preparing sandwiches to carry with you for the next day.
- When planning your Camino, it is important to remember that overnight stays at either end of your trip tend to be the most expensive. Therefore, it is important balance reducing the cost of travel with the cost of extra overnight stays. For example, overnight train journeys in sleepers maybe expensive but when balanced against an overnight stay in Madrid or Barcelona they often work out more cost effective as well as more fun. Equally, the cost of an extra overnight stay in Santiago and taking the bus may contribute to justifying the cost of getting a taxi directly to Sarria.
- If you are short of money, then you should always try and stay in the religious and parish run albergues as these tend to be donativo for both the accommodation and the evening meal. Donativo means donating and you are expected to pay what you can afford which means if you can't afford anything then you don't pay anything. This can be a real boost for pilgrims who otherwise would not be able to afford the pilgrimage but

requires the rest of us to be slightly more generous when staying in these albergues.

# What is the Pilgrim Passport?

The Pilgrim Credential or the Pilgrim Passport as it is more commonly known is a foldable card that you buy at the start of your pilgrimage. The card is designed to be stamped along the way to show you have walked the way. It is also the proof when staying at Albergues that you are a genuine pilgrim (and not just a tourist trying to take advantage of the very cheap pilgrim accommodation). You can get stamps (sellos) for your pilgrim passport at all the albergues along the way as well as most of the churches and cafes. Albergues, cafés, restaurants and churches compete to produce the most attractive and interesting stamps and most pilgrims appear to enjoy collecting the stamps. The pilgrim passport is a great memento of your pilgrimage. The pilgrimage office in Santiago expects that pilgrims who are walking just the last 100km to collect two stamps per for each day, but I am personally unaware of anyone being refused the official certificate of completion (the Compostela) because they missed a stamp on a particular day.

# Example Pilgrim Passport

# Example Compostela Certificate of Completion

Capitulum hujus Almae Apostolicae et Metropolitanae Ecclesiae Compostellanae sigilli Altaris Beati Jacobi Apostoli custos, ut omnibus Fidelibus et Peregrinis ex toto terrarum Orbe, devotionis affectu vel voti causa, ad limina Apostoli Nostri Hispaniarum Patroni ac Tutelaris SANCTI JACOBI convenientibus, authenticas visitationis litteras expediat, omnibus et singulis praesentes inspecturis, notum facit: *Dnum .*

*Marcum McCarthy*

hoc sacratissimum Templum perfecto utique pedibus sive equitando itinere postrema centum millia metrorum, birota vero ducentorum, pietatis causa devote visitasse. In quorum fidem praesentes litteras, sigillo ejusdem Sanctae Ecclesiae munitas, ei confero.

Datum Compostellae die *24* mensis *Iulii* anno Dni *2014*

Segundo L. Pérez López
Deán de la S.A.M.I. Catedral de Santiago

# Where do you get a Pilgrim Passport from?

## Online from the Camino Forum

www.santiagodecompostela.me/products/official-pilgrim-credencial-pilgrim-passport-from-the-pilgrims-office-in-santiago

This is a very convenient and quick option as Ivar who runs the forum mails them out very quickly and at a reasonable price. This is my preferred option.

## Online from APOC (American Pilgrims on the Camino)

www.americanpilgrims.com/camino/credential_req_external.html

There is some very good information about collecting stamps (sellos) on this request page, so it is worth a look even if you don't order from APOC.

## From the Irish Friends of Saint James

Either Online.

www.caminosociety.ie/pilgrim-passports/pass2.324.html

OR....

In person from the sacristy of the Church of St James, James Street, Dublin 8 (GPS Coordinates: 53.34338 -6.28831) (Monday to Friday 10:00 am to 12:00 pm). The church of St James is opposite the world-famous St James's Gate Guinness brewery. The brewery gets its name from the medieval western gate into Dublin which was the traditional starting point of Irish pilgrimages to Santiago. Apparently after getting your Irish pilgrims passport you can visit the brewery and get your first stamp from the Guinness brewery itself. The cost of the Irish pilgrim passport is 10 euro which seems expensive but this money is used to help fund the Irish Friends of St James.

## In Sarria

The pilgrim passport can be purchased from the church of Santa Mariña, Rúa de Maior (open 11 am till 1 pm and 6 pm till 9 pm except Mondays when they are open 7 pm till 8 pm) ( GPS Coordinates: 42.77745, -7.441458)or from the monastery of the Magdalena, Avenida de la Merced, 60 (open 10 am till 1 pm and from 4 pm till 7 pm)( GPS Coordinates: 42.77905, -7.421126) or from the Albergue Credencial ( GPS Coordinates: 42.77497, -7.4091).

# Do you really have to get up at 6 am in the morning?

In the summer months, it is generally too hot to walk between the hours of 1 pm and 7 pm and as a consequence you really need to get all your walking done in the morning. This requires that you set your alarm for about 5:30 and be out walking by 6am. Most cafés along the Camino open especially early to cater for pilgrims and many pilgrims including myself aim to get an hour's walking in before stopping for breakfast. Getting up at 5:30 means you need to be getting to bed by about 9 pm. This may sound unusual, but your body needs as much rest as possible and you will adjust to this schedule very quickly. In the non-summer months, I would strongly advise against walking in the early morning dark. The biggest cause of death on the Camino is from road traffic accidents and it is simply not worth the risk of any road walking while it is still dark.

# How to use the GPS Coordinates

I have given the coordinates in two formats. One format consists of degrees (°), minutes (') and seconds ("). This format is useful for traditional maps. The second format is decimal degrees and can be used in GPS applications such as MAPS.ME, Google Maps or Google Earth. If you have a smartphone or tablet to read this book you will be able to click on the decimal GPS coordinates and this should link to the satellite navigation software, you have on your device. There are many different apps which will work. I will mention two apps which allow off-line use of pre-downloaded maps. These are MAPS.ME from My.com BV and All-in-One Off-line Maps from Psyberia. With both these you can download a complete map of Spain before you leave home. There are new apps arriving all the time, so it is well worth searching Google Play or the App Store for other apps. If you pre-download the maps, the two apps I have mentioned will enable you to use the GPS coordinates from this book to direct you on foot to the door of the hostel without incurring roaming charges.

24

# MAPS.ME Screenshot

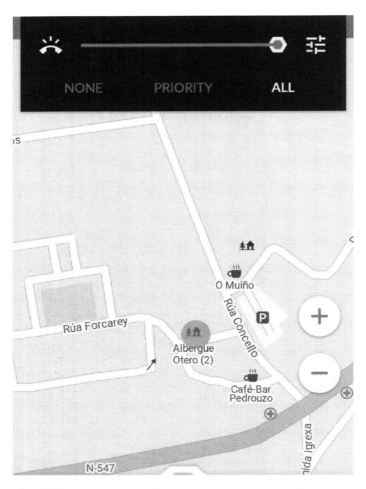

NONE          PRIORITY          ALL

O Muiño

Rúa Forcarey

Rúa Concello

Albergue
Otero (2)

Café-Bar
Pedrouzo

N-547

# Albergue Otero

hostel

1327 km

SHARE

☆
BOOKMARK

ROUTE

# All-in-One Offline Maps Screenshot

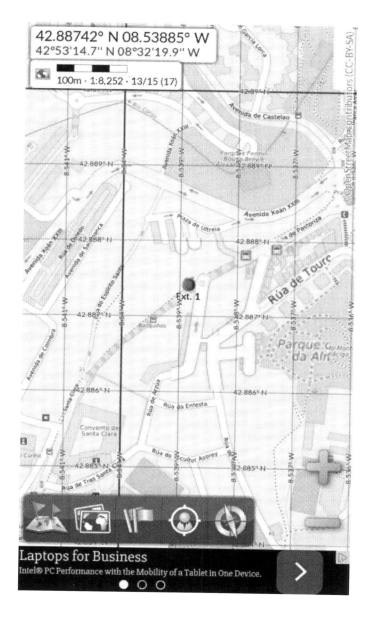

# Estimated walking times

One of the constant frustrations I had during my first Camino was with the distances and the estimated walking times in the current crop of guidebooks. These distances and estimated walking times seem to bear very little similarity to my experience. An ever-present topic of conversation among fellow pilgrims was the "Camino kilometre" which varied in length somewhere between 1.1km and 1.9km. As for the estimated walking times, it was clear that the person who wrote the guidebook I used when I made my first Camino was extremely fit or extremely bad at recording times accurately. In this guide, I want to give you as the reader a realistic expectation of how much time each stretch will take, so that you can make sensible decisions about whether to push on to the next village or stay where you are. I believe that the Camino is best experienced at the pace that your body dictates. I have put a lot of effort into the estimated timings, but they are purely there as an aid to deciding about where you stop for the evening or where you stop for brunch or lunch. In an attempt to give you good ballpark estimates for each stage, I give 3 estimated timings which are based on three walking speeds. The fastest time is based on a what is called a "preferred walking speed" of 5.3 km/hr walking speed, which is roughly the preferred walking speed of a fit person with no backpack on the flat *("preferred walking speed" - research shows that although most people can walk at speeds of up to 7.5 km/hr, we naturally walk at a pace that minimise the amount of energy used for the distance covered and this is in the region of 4.1 to 5.3 km/hr when not encumbered down by a backpack).* The slowest time is 3.9km/hr and is based upon someone who is not super fit and is carrying a backpack on the flat. The middle timing is based on a preferred walking speed of 4.6km/hr on the flat and is roughly equivalent to a normal fit person carrying a backpack on the flat. The timing takes into account the total 3D distance travelled and the effect on walking speed of going up and downhill. (*For more than a 100 years, hikers have relied on Naismith's rule to estimate walking times when the terrain goes up and down. Naismith's rule was improved upon and made into Tobler's rule but it wasn't until 2012 when two Japanese researchers, Yasuhisa Kondo and Yoichi Seino, decided to develop their own rule from scratch using the GPS data from real life hikes that there has been an evidence based calculation available. With Kondo and Seino's calculation it is possible to estimate hiking times over terrain where the slope is constantly changing. I suspect over the next few years there will be further refinements on this method for estimating walking time but for now it is the best method available and has formed the basis for the estimates included in this guide*).

# *Useful Stores on the Camino*

## Sarria

### Peregrinoteca

Calle Benigno Quiroga, 16 - Bajo 27600 Sarria (Lugo)
42.77678,-7.4128
42°46'36"N, 7°24'46"W
+34 9 8253 0190
www.peregrinoteca.com/tienda/

## Santiago

### Decathlon

Calle Polonia Nº2 15707 (414) SANTIAGO
42.90244,-8.5102
42°54'9"N, 8°30'37"W
+34 9 8189 7516

### El Corte Inglés

Rúa do Restollal, 50 15702 Santiago de Compostela, A Coruña
42.8625,-8.54329
42°51'45"N, 8°32'36"W
+34 9 8152 7200

# Chapter 3 - Self-Care on the Camino

## Keeping your fluid intake up

You will lose substantially larger amounts of water than you are used to when walking particularly in the summer. When you lose water to perspiration you also lose two very important salts Sodium Chloride and Potassium Chloride. If either your Potassium or Sodium levels drop too far you will very suddenly feel light headed, you may well faint and if you don't restore your salt levels to normal it can be life threatening especially in the intense heat, so this small section is important. The recommendation is that you carry at least 2 litres of drinking water with you at all times. You should replenish your water bottles at every opportunity. It is advisable to always carry rehydration salts with you. Rehydration salts are sold as diarrhoea rehydration powder. These rehydration salts are expensive, but I would encourage you to carry them if not for yourself then for other pilgrims who may become dehydrated. You can buy soft drinks which have the correct balance of rehydration salts, water and sugar. Coca-Cola market such a product called Aquarius which is sold widely on the Camino. It comes in just two flavours lemon and orange and is not as tasty as the carbonated drinks but is much better for you when you are walking. There are supermarket equivalents which are very similar but much cheaper and if you find they suit you, it is worth buying a couple of litres in the local supermarket in the evening for the next day. One word of caution is that Aquarius contains sugar and therefore is not suitable if you are diabetic. Alternatively, you can drink water for free. If there are no drinking taps available, there is a tradition that anyone who lives on the Camino will always provide water to a thirsty pilgrim. Please remember this is only a tradition and people who live on the Camino have every right to refuse. None the less, this is a tradition which in my experience is observed and the good people who live on the Camino are often quite willing to fill your water bottle. It is likely you will need to increase your use of table salt on your food to balance the amount of sodium you lose through perspiration. This is needed while you are walking such large distances in the heat, but it is important to remember when you get home that additional table salt in your normal diet is bad for your blood pressure. To keep your Potassium levels up the easiest options are bananas, potatoes, beans, mushrooms, pears, fish and yoghurt.

Public water taps come in three types. The safest type is those which have chlorinated water from the town's drinking water supply (aqua potable), the second type is untreated drinking water (fuente natural) which you drink at your own risk, the third (aqua no potable) is guaranteed to be unsafe for drinking.

There are three choices when it comes to carrying water. Firstly, are the specialised water bladders. Even the high-quality water bladders from the likes of Osprey and Camelbak can be purchased on the internet for around €25. If you are going to invest in a water bladder, then it is worth paying for a good quality bladder. A good quality bladder is one that has high quality seams that have been well tested against leaks and that have an in-built flat shape that keeps the water from pooling at the bottom of your backpack. While generally the lower is better when it comes to weight, it is even better that weight is as close to your spine as possible which the shaped bladders ensure. In addition, the shaped bladders minimise any slopping of the water which will have a small but persistent energy zapping effect. Finally, on water bladders, the better-quality bladders are made from anti-microbial materials which will help prevent any nasty bugs finding a home in the water bladder.

The second alternative is the good quality 1 litre lightweight aluminium water cans which can be purchased for about €5 on the internet. These are not quite as handy as the water bladders but pulling out and putting back a fellow pilgrim's water can in their backpack pockets is an extremely social activity that can be the start of a great conversation with a fellow pilgrim and sometimes it can be the start of lifelong friendship.

The third alternative is to simply re-use the plastic water bottles you purchase the water in. They are very light and will normally last a few days or even a week or two. Again, this has the advantage of requiring you to ask a fellow pilgrim for help if you don't want to stop and take your backpack off.

# Feet Care on the Camino

Unless you are a regular walker, on a 100km walk you will develop problems with your feet despite the best boots and the best socks available. As with most things prevention of blisters is much better than cure. Blisters are caused by friction between your sock and your skin. The choice of sock is therefore important. Research has shown that twin layer socks help reduce the incidence of blisters. Most good walking socks have twin layers on the points most likely to rub.

The second risk factor for the friction that causes blisters is moisture, again choosing modern walking socks that are designed to wick moisture away from the skin on your foot is a wise investment. You can also help reduce the risk of blisters by regularly taking your boots or shoes off, changing your socks and letting your feet cool down and dry off.

Finally keep the skin of your feet supple by rubbing off the hard dead skin with a pumice stone. This will allow the skin of your feet to be more flexible and thereby avoid the friction which causes blisters.

In terms of treating blisters, research shows that draining blisters works better than padding them. Draining can be achieved by a method called "threading" or by cutting a hole in the blister. "Threading" is where you thread a needle with cotton and sow the cotton through your blister in order to drain the blister. The thread is left in overnight to ensure that the blister remains drained. However, threading involves significant risk of serious infection even if you apply generous amounts of iodine to the needle, the thread and your foot. It is difficult to do to your own feet and it is painful and I must confess I have done it to myself in the past. However, my very strong recommendation if at all possible is to pay out the €30 consult fee and get a professional to look after your feet. I was extremely lucky on my first Camino that at the point where my feet were so bad that I was at my lowest point on my whole Camino and felt I could go no further that I was joined at the table where I was having lunch by an Irish podiatrist who was a complete stranger. This fellow pilgrim kindly gave me a free consult, patched me up and taught me what I needed to get my feet back in action after two days of rest. Rather than rely on just luck and partly as an expression of gratitude to my podiatric benefactor I am including a list of podiatrists along the way.

(A side note that when buying hiking socks buy the best you can afford, generally only buy hiking socks which are specific for each foot i.e. they are marked with an L and an R)

# List of Podiatrists from Sarria to Santiago

## Sarria

### Clínica Podologica Alvarez
Rúa Diego Pazos, 16
42.778935,-7.411806 42°46'44"N, 7°24'43"W
+34 9 8253 5153

### Podologo Marta Perez
Rúa Calvo Sotelo, 68
42.780905,-7.414375 42°46'51"N, 7°24'52"W
+34 9 8253 4153

## Portomarín

### Clinica del Pie
Calle Diputación 2, Mercado Municipal L9
42.80789,-7.61617 42°48'28"N, 7°36'58"W
+34 6 4445 7966

## Palas de Rei

### Pampin Negro
Avda. de Compostela, 29 Bajo
42.8727,-7.86933 42°52'22"N, 7°52'10"W
+34 9 8238 0121
+34 6 3924 8332

## Santiago

### Clínica Podologica Federico Peñamaría
Rúa de Ramón Cabanillas, 6
42.873267,-8.549901 42°52'24"N, 8°32'60"W
+34 9 8159 8808

### Saleta Becerra Noal
Rúa da República de el Salvador, 28
42.874545,-8.548369 42°52'28"N, 8°32'54"W
+34 9 8157 2388

### Clínica Del Pie Sanjurjo

Rúa de Frei Rosendo Salvado, 10
42.873708,-8.550334 42°52'25"N, 8°33'1"W
+34 9 8159 4020

## Clínica do Pé Óliver Regueiro

Rúa De Madrid, 3 Bajo 2 Fontiñas - Frente A área Central
42.881385,-8.528218 42°52'53"N, 8°31'42"W
+34 9 8159 3918

## Clínica do Pé, Patricia Seoane Iglesias

Rúa de Montero Ríos, 28
42.875646,-8.54705 42°52'32"N, 8°32'49"W
+34 9 8159 3918

## Clínica Riosan Fisioterapia & Podología

Avenida da Mestra Victoria Míguez, 43
42.469684,-8.573684 42°28'11"N, 8°34'25"W
+34 9 8152 2926

## Podóloga - Rocío Dono Gago

Rúa do Restollal, 47
42.863086,-8.542003 42°51'47"N, 8°32'31"W
+34 6 3839 4684

## Podologa Marina Porto Paredes

Galeras, 9 Bajo
42.882914,-8.548765 42°52'58"N, 8°32'56"W
+34 8 8103 1132
www.podologiamarinaporto.es

## Clínica do Pe Manuel Tojo

Calle Doutor Teixeiro 28, 1º
42.874078,-8.545715 42°52'27"N, 8°32'45"W
+34 8 8197 4412
+34 6 8564 7175
www.manueltojopodologo.es

## Secundino Coto Podólogo

Montero Ríos, 33 2º C
42.875403,-8.547803 42°52'31"N, 8°32'52"W
+34 8 8197 7481
+34 6 4927 9076
www.secundinocotopodologo.es

## Cepeda Clinica Podolixica

San Paio de Antealtares, 6 Baixo
42.880857,-8.54286 42°52'51"N, 8°32'34"W
+34 9 8158 5758

## Clínica Del Pie Mª Jose Fernandez

Xeneral Pardiñas, 5 1º B
42.876028,-8.546136 42°52'34"N, 8°32'46"W
+34 9 8193 7565

## Clínica Podoloxica Galastur

Avenida de Lugo, 7 Baixo
42.871986,-8.543973 42°52'19"N, 8°32'38"W
+34 8 8195 9183

## Podologo Garcia Folgar, Rafael

Avenida Rosalía de Castro, 37 1º D
42.87507,-8.55078 42°52'30"N, 8°33'3"W
+34 9 8159 7260

# Chapter 4 - Sarria to Portomarín

## Waypoint Summary Sarria to Portomarín

| From | Waypoint | Decimal GPS | DMS GPS | Distance | 3.9 km/hr | 3.9 km/hr + breaks | 4.6 km/hr | 4.6 km/hr + breaks | 5.3 km/hr | 5.3 km/hr + breaks |
|---|---|---|---|---|---|---|---|---|---|---|
| Sarria | Vilei (Barbadelo) | 42.76897 -7.44426 | 42°46'8"N 7°26'39"W | 3.7km | 1hrs 12mins | 1hrs 26mins | 1hrs 1mins | 1hrs 13mins | 0hrs 53mins | 1hrs 3mins |
| Vilei (Barbadelo) | Barbadelo | 42.76784 -7.45235 | 42°46'4"N 7°27'8"W | 1.0km | 0hrs 19mins | 0hrs 23mins | 0hrs 16mins | 0hrs 19mins | 0hrs 14mins | 0hrs 17mins |
| Barbadelo | Rente | 42.76810 -7.45900 | 42°46'5"N 7°27'32"W | 0.7km | 0hrs 13mins | 0hrs 16mins | 0hrs 11mins | 0hrs 13mins | 0hrs 10mins | 0hrs 12mins |
| Rente | A Serra | 42.77099 -7.46704 | 42°46'16"N 7°28'1"W | 0.7km | 0hrs 15mins | 0hrs 18mins | 0hrs 12mins | 0hrs 15mins | 0hrs 11mins | 0hrs 13mins |
| A Serra | Morgade | 42.78218 -7.52120 | 42°46'56"N 7°31'16"W | 5.9km | 1hrs 48mins | 2hrs 9mins | 1hrs 31mins | 1hrs 49mins | 1hrs 19mins | 1hrs 35mins |
| Morgade | Ferreiros | 42.78364 -7.53266 | 42°47'1"N 7°31'58"W | 1.4km | 0hrs 25mins | 0hrs 30mins | 0hrs 21mins | 0hrs 25mins | 0hrs 18mins | 0hrs 22mins |
| Ferreiros | Mirallos | 42.78380 -7.53627 | 42°47'2"N 7°32'11"W | 0.3km | 0hrs 5mins | 0hrs 6mins | 0hrs 4mins | 0hrs 5mins | 0hrs 3mins | 0hrs 4mins |
| Mirallos | Pena | 42.78541 -7.54262 | 42°47'7"N 7°32'33"W | 0.5km | 0hrs 9mins | 0hrs 11mins | 0hrs 8mins | 0hrs 10mins | 0hrs 7mins | 0hrs 8mins |
| Pena | Mercadoiro | 42.78867 -7.56871 | 42°47'19"N 7°34'7"W | 2.6km | 0hrs 44mins | 0hrs 53mins | 0hrs 38mins | 0hrs 45mins | 0hrs 33mins | 0hrs 39mins |
| Mercadoiro | A Parrocha | 42.79401 -7.58755 | 42°47'38"N 7°35'15"W | 1.7km | 0hrs 30mins | 0hrs 36mins | 0hrs 25mins | 0hrs 30mins | 0hrs 22mins | 0hrs 26mins |
| A Parrocha | Vilachá | 42.79558 -7.60349 | 42°47'44"N 7°36'13"W | 1.3km | 0hrs 22mins | 0hrs 26mins | 0hrs 18mins | 0hrs 22mins | 0hrs 16mins | 0hrs 19mins |
| Vilachá | Portomarín | 42.80457 -7.61655 | 42°48'16"N 7°36'60"W | 1.8km | 0hrs 31mins | 0hrs 38mins | 0hrs 26mins | 0hrs 32mins | 0hrs 23mins | 0hrs 28mins |
| Sarria | Portomarín | 42.80457 -7.61655 | 42°48'16"N 7°36'60"W | 21.6km | 6hrs 37mins | 7hrs 56mins | 5hrs 37mins | 6hrs 44mins | 4hrs 52mins | 5hrs 50mins |

# Sarria to Portomarín
## Elevation Chart

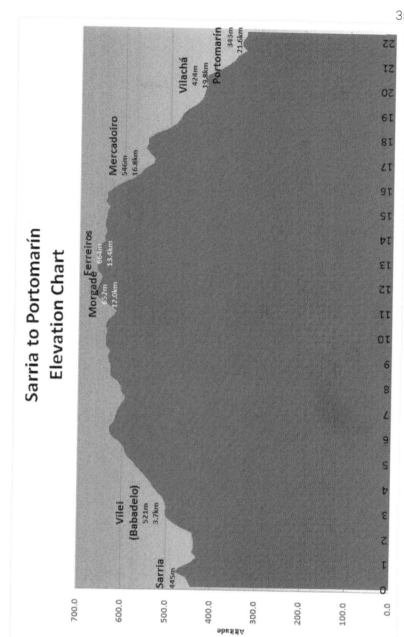

36

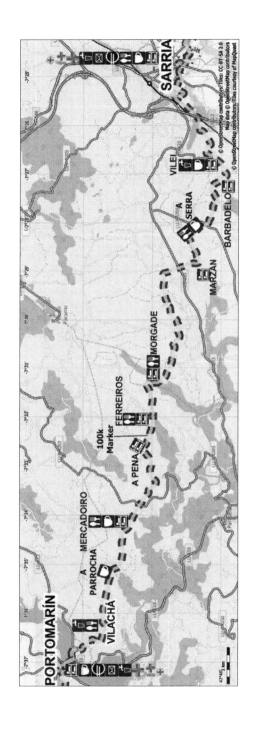

## Notes about Today's Stage

The first part of your first day involves a climb of about 200m over about 5km. This is a moderate climb and you may want to take a break after the first 4km in Vilei (Barbadelo). This is also an ideal opportunity for a morning comfort break before starting the relatively long stretch to Morgade. Remember most albergues will also act as a cafe/bar if there are no dedicated cafe/bars. After Vilei (Barbadelo), you pass by Barbadelo itself about 1km further on. Although there are hamlets on the way, it is another 7km to the next village Morgade. The good news is there is a moderate amount of shade along the route which eases the strain of the climb on a hot day. Morgade is the most popular stop for lunch. After Morgade you will have completed the main climb and the rest of the day is physically less demanding but note that the descent into Portomarín is steep which will slow you down. After Morgade you will pass through Ferreiros which is just before the official 100km marker and offers a good alternative lunch stop to Morgade. After Ferreiros you pass through the tiny hamlet of A Pena and thence to Mercadoiro which I find provides a very pleasant afternoon break. After Mercadoiro you will pass through the tiny hamlet of A Parrocha and finally Vilachá which is less than 2 km from Portomarín.

Without prior training, today, although a relatively short stage, still involves about 7 hours of walking due to the moderately steep climb and descent.

At certain points in Galicia including part of the descent into Portomarin, you will be faced with the option of following two sets of the stone way markers (called mojones in Spanish). One set of markers will carry the distance to Santiago Cathedral and the other set of markers will just say "C. Complementario" which stands for Camino Complementario which means complementary or alternative route. The "C. Complementario" route is always slightly longer but is sometimes the recommended route as it is generally a more pleasant route.

Since 2017, pilgrims now have three choices for the final descent towards Portomarín. The middle route is the "official" measured route but contains at one point a treacherous descent. The right route is the shortest route, but is extremely steep and brings with it the risk of blisters due to the steepness of the descent. The left route adds about 400 metres but is the easiest and most pleasant route.

The final walk into Portomarín is beautiful and takes you across the Belesar dam. As you cross you may be able to see on your left some of the remains of the original village which was flooded with the creation of the dam. The entrance into Portomarín itself is very steep but also very pretty as the archway, the church and several other buildings were relocated stone by stone when Portomarín was relocated as part of the creation of the dam.

# Sarria

114km to Santiago. 3.7km to Vilei. Altitude 443m. Available Beds=820. Local Facilities= CAFE/BAR, RESTAURANT, ATM, HOTEL OR GUEST HOUSE TYPE ACCOMMODATION, PHARMACY, MEDICAL CENTRE, GROCERY STORE. GPS: 42.777181, -7.413777

## Map of Sarria

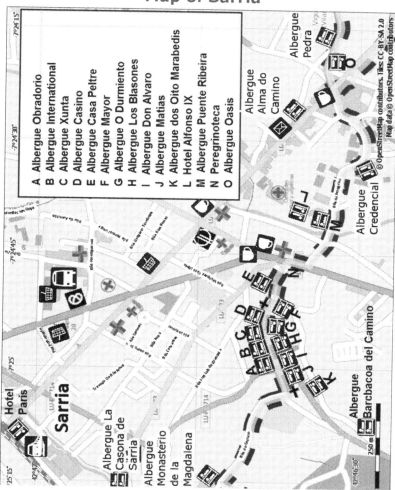

A  Albergue Obradorio
B  Albergue International
C  Albergue Xunta
D  Albergue Casino
E  Albergue Casa Peltre
F  Albergue Mayor
G  Albergue O Durmiento
H  Albergue Los Blasones
I  Albergue Don Alvaro
J  Albergue Matias
K  Albergue dos Oito Marabedis
L  Hotel Alfonso IX
M  Albergue Puente Ribeira
N  Peregrinoteca
O  Albergue Oasis

# Background on Sarria

Sarria probably gets its name from the pre-Roman Seurros tribe that is credited with the founding of the town. However, the town as we now know it had its foundation as a Jacobean (Camino) town in the 12th century when it was refounded as Vilanova de Sarria (Sarria New Town) by King Alfonso IX of Leon (1171-1230). By coincidence Alfonso IX died in Sarria whilst on pilgrimage to Santiago to give thanks for the capture of Merida from the Moors. It was the death of Alfonso IX in Sarria that marked the creation of the country we now know as Spain for his son Ferdinand, who was already King of Castile through marriage, thus became King of the new combined kingdom of Castile and Leon.

The heart of Sarria is Rúa Mayor in the old town where most of the albergues and restaurants are to be found. Here too is the 19th century church of Santa Marina with its charming pilgrim mural on the outside wall. There is a good choice of restaurants including an authentic Italian run by Italians. If in season the Padron Peppers (green peppers grilled or fried in olive oil well seasoned with sea salt) is an absolute delight. The sharpness of the peppers depends on the time within the season, with early season peppers being sweeter and late season peppers carrying more of a punch. There is of course as with everywhere the delicious octopus, but I think this is a delicacy best experienced in the specialist pulperias in Melide. The temptation with so much great fish and seafood is to miss out on the local meat which is also excellent as most of this part of Galicia is dedicated to cattle farming (mainly for dairy but with some great beef as well).

On your exit from Sarria, you will climb up Rúa Maior in the old town. You need to turn first right just after the Italian restaurant. Follow the road until you see the Monastario of Magdalena in front of you. To follow the Camino, turn sharp left here. However, Monastario of Magdalena dates from the 13th century. The monastery was founded by two Italian pilgrims originally as a pilgrim hostel and it is now once again acting as an albergue. It is well worth the 20 metre detour to visit even if it is just to get your first passport stamp of the day.

After turning left, you head downhill for about 250 metres, then turn right and carry on the road for about 200 metres before turning left and crossing a small stone bridge. Please note that the railway line that you cross, although not busy, is still in use so you must look both ways before crossing. The climb up to Vilei is probably the steepest climb of the day so please don't be discouraged if it feels really tough.

# Pilgrim Accommodation Sarria

## Albergue Xunta
Address: Calle Mayor, 79
GPS Coordinates: 42.77748, -7.414881 / 42°46'39"N, 7°24'54"W
Telephone: +34 6 6039 6813
Web: camino.xacobeo.es/albergues/albergue-de-sarria
Min Cost= €6, No of Beds = 41, Facilities= KITCHEN, WASHING
MACHINE, TUMBLE DRYER
Opening Times: 13:00 till 23:00 January 1 till December 31

## Albergue Alma del Camino
Address: Rúa de Calvo Sotelo, 199
GPS Coordinates: 42.77641, -7.40742 / 42°46'35"N, 7°24'27"W
Telephone: +34 9 8287 6768 OR +34 6 2982 2036
Email: sarria@almadocamino.com
Web: www.almadelcamino.com
Min Cost= €6.5, No of Beds = 100, Facilities= KITCHEN, WASHING
MACHINE, TUMBLE DRYER, BICYCLE STORAGE, INTERNET
Opening Times: 11:30 till 23:00 February 15 till December 15
Booking.com: www.booking.com/hotel/es/albergue-alma-do-camino.html

## Albergue Puente Ribeira
Address: Rúa do Peregrino, 23
GPS Coordinates: 42.77584, -7.41161 / 42°46'33"N, 7°24'42"W
Telephone: +34 9 8287 6789 OR +34 6 9817 5619
Email: info@alberguepunteribeira.com
Web: www.alberguepunteribeira.com
Min Cost= €7, No of Beds = 50, Facilities= WASHING MACHINE,
TUMBLE DRYER, BICYCLE STORAGE, INTERNET PRIVATE ROOMS
AVAILABLE
Opening Times: 11:00 till 23:00 March 1 till October 31
Booking.com: www.booking.com/hotel/es/albergue-puente-ribeira.html

## Albergue Obradorio
Address: Calle Mayor, 49
GPS Coordinates: 42.77741, -7.415545 / 42°46'39"N, 7°24'56"W
Telephone: +34 9 8253 2442 OR +34 6 4720 9267
Email: reservas@albergueobradoirosarria.es
Web: www.albergueobradoirosarria.es
Min Cost= €7, No of Beds = 38, Facilities= WASHING MACHINE,
TUMBLE DRYER, BICYCLE STORAGE, INTERNET
Opening Times: 11:00 till 23:00 Holy Week till October 31

Booking.com: www.booking.com/hotel/es/obradoiro-sarria.es.html

## Albergue Barbacoa del Camino

Address: Calle Esqueiredos,1
GPS Coordinates: 42.77431, -7.41967 / 42°46'28"N, 7°25'11"W
Telephone: +34 6 1987 9476
Web: www.facebook.com/alberguebarbacoa
Min Cost= €8, No of Beds = 18, Facilities=
Opening Times: 11:00 till 23:00 March 1 till October 31

## Albergue Don Alvaro

Address: Calle Mayor, 10
GPS Coordinates: 42.7771, -7.41667 / 42°46'38"N, 7°25'0"W
Telephone: +34 9 8253 1592 OR +34 6 8646 8803
Web: www.alberguedonalvaro.com
Min Cost= €9, No of Beds = 40, Facilities= KITCHEN
Opening Times: 12:00 till 23:00 January 1 till December 31
Booking.com: www.booking.com/hotel/es/albergue-casa-don-alvaro-sarria.html

## Albergue Matías

Address: Calle Mayor, 4
GPS Coordinates: 42.77691, -7.4172 / 42°46'37"N, 7°25'2"W
Telephone: +34 9 8253 4285
Email: anuman43@hotmail.com
Min Cost= €9, No of Beds = 37, Facilities= WASHING MACHINE,
TUMBLE DRYER, INTERNET, PRIVATE ROOMS AVAILABLE
Opening Times: 11:00 till 22:30 January 1 till December 31

## Albergue Casino

Address: Calle Mayor, 65
GPS Coordinates: 42.77744, -7.41475 / 42°46'39"N, 7°24'53"W
Telephone: +34 9 8288 6785
Email: atencionalcliente@alberguecasino.com
Web: www.alberguecasino.com
Min Cost= €9, No of Beds = 28, Facilities= KITCHEN, WASHING
MACHINE, TUMBLE DRYER, BICYCLE STORAGE
Opening Times: 11:30 till 23:00 March 1 till October 31

## Albergue Credencial

Address: Rúa do Peregrino, 50
GPS Coordinates: 42.77497, -7.4091 / 42°46'30"N, 7°24'33"W
Telephone: +34 9 8287 6455
Email: alberguecredencial@gmail.com
Web: www.facebook.com/alberguecredencial

Min Cost= €9, No of Beds = 28, Facilities= WASHING MACHINE, TUMBLE DRYER, BICYCLE STORAGE, INTERNET
Opening Times: 09:30 till 23:30 January 1 till December 31
Booking.com: www.booking.com/hotel/es/albergue-credencial.html

## Albergue A Pedra

Address: Camino Vigo, 19
GPS Coordinates: 42.776398, -7.40606 / 42°46'35"N, 7°24'22"W
Telephone: +34 9 8253 0130 OR +34 6 5251 7199
Email: info@albergueapedra.com
Web: www.albergueapedra.com
Min Cost= €9, No of Beds = 15, Facilities= KITCHEN, WASHING MACHINE, TUMBLE DRYER, BICYCLE STORAGE, INTERNET
Opening Times: 11:00 till 23:00 March 1 till November 30
Booking.com: www.booking.com/hotel/es/albergue-a-pedra.html

## Albergue Monasterio de la Magadalena

Address: Avenida de la Merced,60
GPS Coordinates: 42.77905, -7.421126 / 42°46'45"N, 7°25'16"W
Telephone: +34 9 8253 3568 OR +34 8 1568 8521
Email: sarria@alberguesdelcamino.com
Web: www.alberguesdelcamino.com
Min Cost= €10, No of Beds = 100, Facilities= KITCHEN, WASHING MACHINE, INTERNET
Opening Times: 11:00 till 23:00 March 1 till October 31
Booking.com: www.booking.com/hotel/es/albergue-monasterio-de-la-magdalena.en-gb.html

## Albergue Granxa de Barreiros

Address: Carretera Sarria-Portomarín, km 54
GPS Coordinates: 42.782772, -7.459864 / 42°46'58"N, 7°27'36"W
Telephone: +34 9 8253 3656 OR +34 6 9812 9000
Email: info@granxadebarreiros.com
Web: www.alberguesarria.com
Min Cost= €10, No of Beds = 49, Facilities= WASHING MACHINE, TUMBLE DRYER, BICYCLE STORAGE, INTERNET
Opening Times: 11:00 till N/A January 1 till October 31

## Albergue Internacional

Address: Calle Mayor, 57
GPS Coordinates: 42.78082, -7.41414 / 42°46'51"N, 7°24'51"W
Telephone: +34 9 8253 5109
Email: info@albergueinternacionalsarria.es
Web: www.albergueinternacionalsarria.es

Min Cost= €10, No of Beds = 43, Facilities= WASHING MACHINE, PRIVATE ROOMS AVAILABLE
Opening Times: 12:00 till 23:00 January 1 till October 31
Booking.com: www.booking.com/hotel/es/albergue-internacional.es.html

## Albergue Los Blasones

Address: Calle Mayor, 31
GPS Coordinates: 42.777455, -7.416034 / 42°46'39"N, 7°24'58"W
Telephone: +34 9 8253 0666 OR +34 6 0051 2565
Web: www.alberguelosblasones.com
Min Cost= €10, No of Beds = 42, Facilities= KITCHEN, WASHING MACHINE, TUMBLE DRYER, BICYCLE STORAGE
Opening Times: 11:00 till 23:00 March 1 till November 30
Booking.com: www.booking.com/hotel/es/albergue-los-blasones.es.html

## Albergue O Durmiñento

Address: Calle Mayor, 44
GPS Coordinates: 42.77739, -7.41516 / 42°46'39"N, 7°24'55"W
Telephone: +34 9 8253 1099 OR +34 6 0086 2508
Email: durmiento_sarria@hotmail.com
Web: albergueodurminento.com
Min Cost= €10, No of Beds = 41, Facilities= WASHING MACHINE, TUMBLE DRYER, BICYCLE STORAGE, INTERNET
Opening Times: 11:00 till 23:00 April 1 till November 30
Booking.com: www.booking.com/hotel/es/albergue-o-durminento.html

## Albergue Las Casona

Address: Rúa San Lázaro, 24
GPS Coordinates: 42.78107, -7.42082 / 42°46'52"N, 7°25'15"W
Telephone: +34 9 8253 5556 OR +34 6 7003 6444
Email: info@lacasonadesarria.es
Web: www.lacasonadesarria.es
Min Cost= €10, No of Beds = 31, Facilities= WASHING MACHINE, TUMBLE DRYER, BICYCLE STORAGE, INTERNET, PRIVATE ROOMS AVAILABLE
Opening Times: 12:00 till 23:00 January 1 till December 31

## Albergue San Lazaro

Address: Calle San Lázaro, 7
GPS Coordinates: 42.780763, -7.419827 / 42°46'51"N, 7°25'11"W
Telephone: +34 9 8253 0626 OR +34 6 5918 5482
Email: alberguesanlazaro@hotmail.com

Web: www.alberguesanlazaro.com
Min Cost= €10, No of Beds = 30, Facilities= KITCHEN, WASHING MACHINE, TUMBLE DRYER, BICYCLE STORAGE, INTERNET, PRIVATE ROOMS AVAILABLE
Opening Times: 12:00 till 23:00 April 1 till October 31
Booking.com: www.booking.com/hotel/es/albergue-san-lazaro.html

## Albergue Oasis

Address: Camino de Santiago a Tricastela, 12
GPS Coordinates: 42.77587, -7.40529 / 42°46'33"N, 7°24'19"W
Telephone: +34 9 8253 5516 OR +34 6 0594 8644
Email: reservas@albergueoasis.com
Web: www.albergueoasis.com
Min Cost= €10, No of Beds = 27, Facilities= KITCHEN, BICYCLE STORAGE, INTERNET
Opening Times: 11:30 till 23:00 March 1 till October 31
Booking.com: www.booking.com/hotel/es/albergue-oasis.html

## Albergue Dos Oito Marabedis

Address: Calle Conde de Lemos, 23
GPS Coordinates: 42.77634, -7.417495 / 42°46'35"N, 7°25'3"W
Telephone: +34 6 2946 1770 OR +34 6 1874 8777
Web: www.alberguedosoitomarabedis.com
Min Cost= €10, No of Beds = 24, Facilities=
Opening Times: 13:00 till 23:00 May 1 till October 31

## Albergue Casa Peltre

Address: Escalinata da Fonte, 10
GPS Coordinates: 42.77687, -7.4133 / 42°46'37"N, 7°24'48"W
Telephone: +34 6 0622 6067 OR +34 6 0622 6067
Email: hola@alberguecasapeltre.es
Web: www.casapeltre.es
Min Cost= €10, No of Beds = 22, Facilities= KITCHEN, WASHING MACHINE, BICYCLE STORAGE, INTERNET
Opening Times: 11:00 till 22:30 April 1 till October 31

## Albergue Mayor

Address: Calle Mayor, 64
GPS Coordinates: 42.77709, -7.41404 / 42°46'38"N, 7°24'51"W
Telephone: +34 6 8514 8474 OR +34 6 4642 7734
Email: alberguemayor@gmail.com
Web: www.alberguemayor.es
Min Cost= €10, No of Beds = 16, Facilities= KITCHEN, WASHING MACHINE, TUMBLE DRYER, BICYCLE STORAGE, INTERNET

Opening Times: 11:00 till 23:00 March 1 till October 31
Booking.com: www.booking.com/hotel/es/albergue-mayor.html

# Vilei

110km to Santiago. 1km to Barbadelo. Altitude 522m. Available
Beds=84. Local Facilities= CAFE/BAR. GPS: 42.768658, -7.444299

## Vilei Village Map

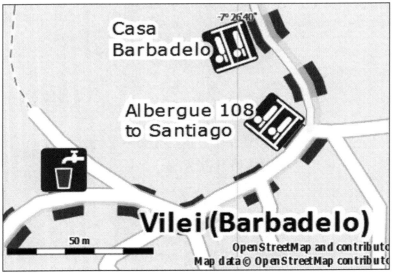

## Notes on Vilei

The cafe at the guest house Casa Barbadelo provides a
welcome first break of the day and has a nice souvenir shop.

## Pilgrim Accommodation Vilei

### Albergue 108 to Santiago

Address: Km 108, Vilei (Barbadelo)
GPS Coordinates: 42.76885, -7.44422 / 42°46'8"N, 7°26'39"W
Telephone: +34 6 3489 4524
Email: albergue108tosantiago@hotmail.com
Web: www.facebook.com/108tosantiago
Min Cost= €8, No of Beds = 14, Facilities= WASHING MACHINE,
TUMBLE DRYER, BICYCLE STORAGE, INTERNET
Opening Times: N/A till N/A January 1 till December 31
Booking.com: www.booking.com/hotel/es/108-to-santiago.html

## Albergue Casa Barbadelo

Address: Vilei
GPS Coordinates: <u>42.76914, -7.44448</u> / 42°46'9"N, 7°26'40"W
Telephone: <u>+34 9 8253 1934</u> OR <u>+34 6 5916 0498</u>
Email: <u>info@bardelo.com</u>
Web: <u>www.barbadelo.com</u>
Min Cost= €9, No of Beds = 70, Facilities= WASHING MACHINE, TUMBLE DRYER, INTERNET, SWIMMING POOL, PRIVATE ROOMS AVAILABLE
Opening Times: 12:00 till N/A Holy Week till October 31
Booking.com: <u>www.booking.com/hotel/es/casa-barbadelo.html</u>

# Barbadelo

109km to Santiago. 0.7km to Rente. Altitude 548m. Available Beds=58. Local Facilities= CAFE/BAR. GPS: <u>42.765867, -7.450292</u>

## Barbadelo Village Map

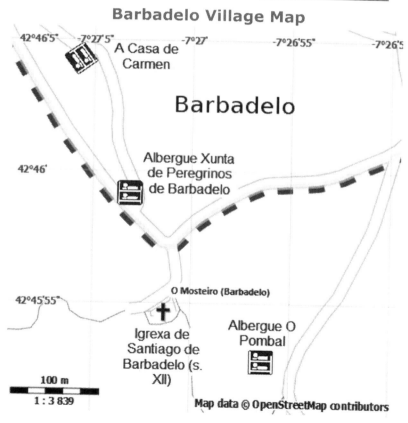

# Notes on Barbadelo

Barbadelo is a small village now but was important enough (along with Portomarín, Palas de Rey, Leboreiro, Boente, Castaneda, and Ferreiros) to be mentioned in the Codex Calixtinus (The Codex Calixtinus is a 12th century manuscript which is regarded as the first ever guidebook for the Camino, in fact it is regarded as the first ever guidebook in Europe). At that time, the village had a monastery dependent on the large abbey at Samos. All that remains of its former importance is the 12th century Romanesque church of Santiago de Barbadelo.

# Pilgrim Accommodation Barbadelo

## Albergue Xunta
Address: Old school, Vilei
GPS Coordinates: 42.76623, -7.45081 / 42°45'58"N, 7°27'3"W
Telephone: +34 6 6039 6814
Web: camino.xacobeo.es/albergues/albergue-de-barbadelo
Min Cost= €6, No of Beds = 18, Facilities= WASHING MACHINE, TUMBLE DRYER
Opening Times: 13:00 till 23:00 January 1 till December 31

## Albergue A Casa de Carmen
Address: San Silvestre
GPS Coordinates: 42.76788, -7.45134 / 42°46'4"N, 7°27'5"W
Telephone: +34 9 8253 2294 OR +34 6 0615 6705
Email: albergueacasadecarmen@gmail.com
Web: www.acasadecarmen.es
Min Cost= €10, No of Beds = 32, Facilities= COMMUNAL MEAL, PRIVATE ROOMS AVAILABLE
Opening Times: 13:00 till 23:00 April 1 till October 31

## Albergue O Pombal
Address: Close to the Church
GPS Coordinates: 42.76469, -7.44889 / 42°45'53"N, 7°26'56"W
Telephone: +34 6 8671 8732
Email: alberguepombal@gmail.com
Web: www.alberguepombal.blogspot.co.uk
Min Cost= €10, No of Beds = 8, Facilities= KITCHEN, WASHING MACHINE, TUMBLE DRYER
Opening Times: 13:00 till 23:00 Holy Week till October 31

## Casa Albergue Molino de Marzán
Address: km 104.5, Marzán (Barbadelo)
GPS Coordinates: 42.7723, -7.48155 / 42°46'20"N, 7°28'54"W

Telephone: <u>+34 6 7943 8077</u>
Email: <u>adm@molinomarzan.com</u>
Web: <u>www.molinomarzan.com</u>
Min Cost= €10, No of Beds = 16, Facilities= KITCHEN, WASHING MACHINE, TUMBLE DRYER, BICYCLE STORAGE, INTERNET
Opening Times: 12:00 till 22:00 March 1 till October 31

# Rente

108km to Santiago. 0.7km to A Serra. Altitude 594m. Local Facilities= HOTEL OR GUEST HOUSE TYPE ACCOMMODATION. GPS: <u>42.76810,-7.45900</u>

# A Serra

108km to Santiago. 5.9km to Morgade. Altitude 630m. Local Facilities= CAFE/BAR. GPS: <u>42.77099, -7.46704</u>

# Morgade

102km to Santiago. 1.4km to Ferreiros. Altitude 651m. Available Beds=16. Local Facilities= CAFE/BAR, RESTAURANT. GPS: <u>42.78215, -7.521219</u>

## Notes on Morgade

Casa Morgade provides an excellent lunch break. The made to order omelettes are good and the toilets provide a truly welcome comfort break especially for female pilgrims.

## Morgade Village Map

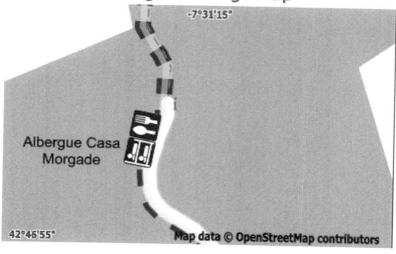

# Pilgrim Accommodation Morgade

## Albergue Casa Morgade

Address: Morgade
GPS Coordinates: <u>42.75212, -7.52122</u> / 42°45'8"N, 7°31'16"W
Telephone: <u>+34 9 8253 1250</u>
Web: <u>www.casamorgade.com</u>
Min Cost= €10, No of Beds = 16, Facilities= WASHING MACHINE,
TUMBLE DRYER, PRIVATE ROOMS AVAILABLE
Opening Times: 12:00 till 23:00 Holy Week till October 31

# Ferreiros

100km to Santiago. 0.3km to Mirallos. Altitude 660m. Available
Beds=34. Local Facilities= RESTAURANT. GPS: <u>42.783159, -
7.532756</u>

## Ferreiros Village Map

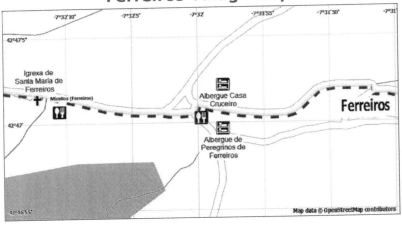

## Notes on Ferreiros

Ferreiros translates as blacksmiths as this was originally the
location where pilgrims on horseback could get the blacksmith to re-
shod their horses.

As Ferreiros is about 700 metres from the 100km marker, some
pilgrims (especially those on escorted tours) will start their pilgrimage
from here rather than Sarria.

Both Casa Cruceiros and O Mirallos are good alternative lunch
breaks. Perhaps not quite to the standard of Casa Morgade but none
the less very good places for a lunch break.

# Pilgrim Accommodation Ferreiros

## Albergue Xunta

Address: Ferreiros
GPS Coordinates: 42.78318, -7.53283 / 42°46'59"N, 7°31'58"W
Telephone: +34 9 8215 7496 OR +34 6 3896 2809
Web: camino.xacobeo.es/albergues/albergue-de-ferreiros
Min Cost= €6, No of Beds = 22, Facilities= KITCHEN, WASHING MACHINE, TUMBLE DRYER, BICYCLE STORAGE.
Opening Times: 13:00 till 23:00 January 1 till December 31

## Albergue Casa Cruceiro

Address: km 100.746
GPS Coordinates: 42.784, -7.53289 / 42°47'2"N, 7°31'58"W
Telephone: +34 9 8254 1240 OR +34 6 3902 0064
Email: casacruceirodeferreiros@gmail.com
Web: www.casacruceirodeferreiros.com
Min Cost= €10, No of Beds = 12, Facilities= WASHING MACHINE, TUMBLE DRYER, PRIVATE ROOMS AVAILABLE
Opening Times: 11:30 till 00:00 March 1 till November 30

# Mirallos

100km to Santiago. 0.5km to A Pena. Altitude 638m. Available Beds=20. Local Facilities= NONE. GPS: 42.783797, -7.536523

## Notes on Mirallos

Mirallos houses the small but elegant 12th century Romanesque church of Santa María de Ferreiros. Originally situated in Ferreiros it was moved stone by stone to its current location in 1790 following a change in the path of the Camino. Like many churches on the Camino it has a beautifully kept walled cemetery attached.

## Pilgrim Accommodation Mirallos

### Albergue O Mirallos

Address: Mirallos
GPS Coordinates: 42.78375, -7.5363 / 42°47'1"N, 7°32'11"W
Telephone: +34 9 8215 7162 OR +34 6 3901 0696
Email: omirallosmanuel@gmail.com
Min Cost= €Donativo, No of Beds = 20, Facilities= BICYCLE STORAGE, INTERNET
Opening Times: N/A till 22:00 January 1 till December 31

# A Pena

100km to Santiago. 2.6km to Mercadoiro. Altitude 644m. Available Beds=6. Local Facilities= NONE. GPS: 42.785413, -7.542627

## A Pena Village Map

## Pilgrim Accommodation A Pena

Address: A Pena, 4
GPS Coordinates: 42.78517, -7.54228 / 42°47'7"N, 7°32'32"W
Telephone: +34 9 8216 7812 OR +34 6 2697 0788
Email: casadoregopena@gmail.com
Web: www.casadorego.com
Min Cost= €10, No of Beds = 6, Facilities= WASHING MACHINE, BICYCLE STORAGE, INTERNET, COMMUNAL MEAL, PRIVATE ROOMS AVAILABLE
Opening Times: 11:00 till 22:00 Holy Week till October 31

# Mercadorio

97km to Santiago. 3.1km to Vilachá. Altitude 547m. Available Beds=34. Local Facilities= CAFE/BAR, RESTAURANT. GPS: 42.788732, -7.568662

## Mercadoiro Village Map
-7°34'10"

42°47'20"

Albergue
Mercadoiro

# Mercadoiro

**Map data © OpenStreetMap contributors**

## Pilgrim Accommodation Mercadorio

### Albergue Mercadoiro
Address: Aldea de Mercadoiro, 2 (km 95.3)
GPS Coordinates: 42.78522, -7.56884 / 42°47'7"N, 7°34'8"W
Telephone: +34 9 8253 1250
Email: canillasfuentes@hotmail.com
Web: www.mercadoiro.com
Min Cost= €10, No of Beds = 34, Facilities= WASHING MACHINE, TUMBLE DRYER, BICYCLE STORAGE, INTERNET, PRIVATE ROOMS AVAILABLE
Opening Times: N/A till N/A March 1 till November 15
Booking.com: www.booking.com/hotel/es/mercadoiro.es.html

# Vilachá

94km to Santiago. 1.8km to Portomarín. Altitude 424m. Available Beds=0. Local Facilities= RESTAURANT, CAFÉ/BAR. GPS: 42.795613, -7.603533

## Notes on Vilachá

Vilachá used to be home to the nice Albergue Casa Banderas which closed down due to the ill health of the owner. Currently the only facility in Vilachá is a vegetarian restaurant which doubles as a nice bar and pleasant last stop before Portomarín.

# Portomarín

92km to Santiago. 7.7km to Gonzar. Altitude 388m. Available
Beds=441. Local Facilities= CAFE/BAR, RESTAURANT, ATM, HOTEL
OR GUEST HOUSE TYPE ACCOMMODATION, PHARMACY, MEDICAL
CENTRE, GROCERY STORE. GPS: 42.807682, -7.615704

## Notes on Portomarín

If water levels are low, you can see parts of the submerged old
town on your left as you cross the long bridge into Portomarín. The
current bridge is from the 1960s but there has been a bridge here since
Roman times.

The creation in 1963 of the reservoir of Belesar, on the river Miño,
flooded the old village of Portomarín. Its main historic buildings were
rescued and moved stone by stone to the new relocated village still
known as Portomarín. These included the 10th century Romanesque
church of San Pedro and the 12th century fortress church of San
Nicolás which is now in the main square and it is here that most
evenings the Pilgrim Mass is said. If you look carefully on parts of both
the inside and outside of the church you can still see the numbering of
the stones which was used to ensure the correct reconstruction of the
church.

Although this is one of the few wine growing regions on this part
of the Camino, Portomarín is more famous for its Aguardente liquor
called Orujo which is normally drunk as a digestive and for which
Portomarín hosts an annual fiesta on Easter Sunday.

Because there are no villages with albergues within easy distance
of either side of Portomarín, Portomarín is often fully booked. It is best
to avoid this situation by booking at least a few days in advance.
However, if you do find yourself in this difficult situation, the town hall,
which is in the main square, will open a sports hall or primary school
and allow you to sleep on the floor overnight.

When leaving in the morning there are very few cafe/bars open for
breakfast. One of the few that does open for breakfast is the Albergue
O Mirador which consequently can become extremely busy. However,
it is worth waiting and taking breakfast here since the next rest stop
with a cafe/bar is over 8km away.

The first kilometre or two of today's hike out of Portomarín is well
shaded but it is the steepest part of today's climb. Fortunately, the
steepness eases off as you exit the woods.

# Portomarín Village Map

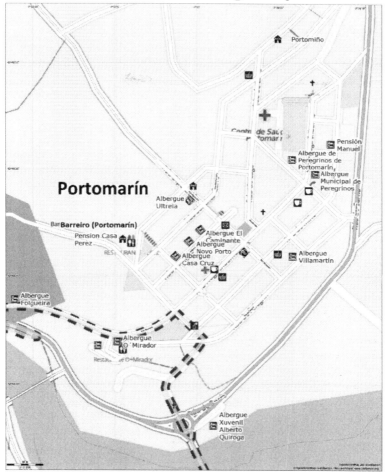

# Pilgrim Accommodation Portomarín

## Albergue Xunta

Address: Carretera de Lugo
GPS Coordinates: 42.80843, -7.61496 / 42°48'30"N, 7°36'54"W
Telephone: +34 9 8254 5143 OR +34 6 6039 6816
Web: camino.xacobeo.es/albergues/albergue-de-portomarin
Min Cost= €6, No of Beds = 114, Facilities= KITCHEN, WASHING MACHINE, TUMBLE DRYER
Opening Times: 13:00 till 22:00 January 1 till December 31

## Albergue Ferramentiero

Address: Calle Chantada, 3
GPS Coordinates: 42.8062, -7.6182 / 42°48'22"N, 7°37'6"W
Telephone: +34 9 8254 5362
Email: info@albergueferramenteiro.com
Web: www.albergueferramenteiro.com
Min Cost= €10, No of Beds = 130, Facilities= KITCHEN, WASHING MACHINE, TUMBLE DRYER, BICYCLE STORAGE, INTERNET
Opening Times: 12:00 till 23:00 Holy Week till October 31
Booking.com: www.booking.com/hotel/es/albergue-ferramenteiro.es.html

## Albergue Folgueira

Address: Avenida de Chantada, 18
GPS Coordinates: 42.8066, -7.61975 / 42°48'24"N, 7°37'11"W
Telephone: +34 9 8254 5166 OR +34 6 5944 5651
Email: info@alberguefolgueira.com
Web: alberguefolgueira.com
Min Cost= €10, No of Beds = 32, Facilities= KITCHEN, WASHING MACHINE, TUMBLE DRYER, BICYCLE STORAGE, INTERNET
Opening Times: 10:00 till 23:00 January 1 till December 31
Booking.com: www.booking.com/hotel/es/albergue-folgueira.es.html

## Albergue Pasiño a Pasiño

Address: Rúa de Compostela, 25
GPS Coordinates: 42.80685, -7.61654 / 42°48'25"N, 7°36'60"W
Telephone: +34 6 6566 7243
Email: alberguepasoapaso@gmail.com
Web: pasinapasin.es
Min Cost= €10, No of Beds = 30, Facilities= KITCHEN, WASHING MACHINE, TUMBLE DRYER, BICYCLE STORAGE, INTERNET
Opening Times: 12:00 till 23:00 January 1 till December 31

## Albergue O Mirador

Address: Rúa do Pelegrín, 27
GPS Coordinates: 42.80618, -7.61802 / 42°48'22"N, 7°37'5"W
Telephone: +34 9 8254 5323
Email: info@omiradorportomarin.com
Web: www.omiradorportomarin.com
Min Cost= €10, No of Beds = 29, Facilities= WASHING MACHINE, TUMBLE DRYER, BICYCLE STORAGE, INTERNET, PRIVATE ROOMS AVAILABLE
Opening Times: 12:00 till 23:00 January 1 till December 31

## Albergue Novo Porto

Address: Calle Benigno Quiroga, 12
GPS Coordinates: 42.80722, -7.61688 / 42°48'26"N, 7°37'1"W
Telephone: +34 9 8254 5277 OR +34 6 1043 6736
Email: novoportoalbergue@gmail.com
Web: alberguenovoporto.com
Min Cost= €10, No of Beds = 22, Facilities= KITCHEN, WASHING
MACHINE, TUMBLE DRYER, INTERNET
Opening Times: 10:00 till 23:30 April 1 till November 30

## Albergue Villamartin

Address: Rúa dos Peregrino, 11
GPS Coordinates: 42.80716, -7.61492 / 42°48'26"N, 7°36'54"W
Telephone: +34 9 8254 5054
Email: reservas@hotelvillajardin.com
Web: www.alberguevillamartin.es
Min Cost= €10, No of Beds = 22, Facilities= KITCHEN, WASHING
MACHINE, TUMBLE DRYER, INTERNET
Opening Times: 12:00 till 23:00 April 1 till October 31

## Albergue Casa Cruz

Address: Calle Benigno Quiroga, 16
GPS Coordinates: 42.80714, -7.61698 / 42°48'26"N, 7°37'1"W
Telephone: +34 9 8254 5140 OR +34 6 5220 4548
Email: info@casacruzportomarin.com
Web: www.casacruzportomarin.com
Min Cost= €10, No of Beds = 16, Facilities= WASHING MACHINE,
TUMBLE DRYER, BICYCLE STORAGE, INTERNET
Opening Times: N/A till 23:00 January 1 till December 31

## Albergue Manuel

Address: Rúa do Miño, 1
GPS Coordinates: 42.80866, -7.61437 / 42°48'31"N, 7°36'52"W
Telephone: +34 9 8254 5385
Email: pensionmanuel1@gmail.com
Web: www.pensionmanuel.es
Min Cost= €10, No of Beds = 16, Facilities= KITCHEN, WASHING
MACHINE, TUMBLE DRYER, BICYCLE STORAGE, INTERNET
Opening Times: 12:00 till N/A April 1 till November 30

## Albergue Porto Santiago

Address: Calle Diputación, 8
GPS Coordinates: 42.80807, -7.61678 / 42°48'29"N, 7°37'0"W
Telephone: +34 6 1882 6515
Email: info@albergueportosantiago.com

Web: www.albergueportosantiago.com
Min Cost= €10, No of Beds = 14, Facilities= KITCHEN, WASHING
MACHINE, TUMBLE DRYER, BICYCLE STORAGE, INTERNET
Opening Times: 12:00 till 23:00 January 1 till December 31

## Albergue Ultreia

Address: Calle Diputación, 9
GPS Coordinates: 42.80796, -7.61672 / 42°48'29"N, 7°37'0"W
Telephone: +34 9 8254 5067 OR +34 6 7660 7292
Email: info@ultreiaportomarin.com
Web: www.ultreiaportomarin.com
Min Cost= €10, No of Beds = 14, Facilities= KITCHEN, WASHING
MACHINE, TUMBLE DRYER, BICYCLE STORAGE, INTERNET
Opening Times: 11:00 till 23:00 January 1 till December 31

## Albergue El Caminante

Address: Calle Benigno Quiroga, 6
GPS Coordinates: 42.80744, -7.61658 / 42°48'27"N, 7°36'60"W
Telephone: +34 9 8254 5176
Email: pension_elcaminante@hotmail.com
Web: pensionelcaminante.com
Min Cost= €10, No of Beds = 12, Facilities= WASHING MACHINE,
TUMBLE DRYER, BICYCLE STORAGE, INTERNET, PRIVATE ROOMS
AVAILABLE
Opening Times: 12:00 till 00:00 Holy Week till October 31

## Albergue Aqua

Address: Calle Barreiros, 2
GPS Coordinates: 42.80745, -7.61824 / 42°48'27"N, 7°37'6"W
Telephone: +34 6 0892 1372
Email: info@aquarooms.es
Web: www.aquarooms.es
Min Cost= €10, No of Beds = 10, Facilities= KITCHEN, WASHING
MACHINE, TUMBLE DRYER, BICYCLE STORAGE, INTERNET, PRIVATE
ROOMS AVAILABLE
Opening Times: 13:00 till 22:00 March 1 till October 31
Booking.com: www.booking.com/hotel/es/albergue-aqua-
portomarin.html

## Casa Marabillas

Address: Camiño do Monte, 3
GPS Coordinates: 42.81009, -7.61586 / 42°48'36"N, 7°36'57"W
Telephone: +34 7 4445 0425 OR +34 9 8218 9086
Email: casadomarabillas@gmail.com
Web: www.casadomarabillas.com

Min Cost= €15, No of Beds = 10, Facilities= KITCHEN, WASHING MACHINE, TUMBLE DRYER, BICYCLE STORAGE, INTERNET
Opening Times: N/A till N/A January 1 till December 31

## Albergue A Fontana De Luxo

Address: Fontedagra 2
GPS Coordinates: 42.80107, -7.61709 / 42°48'4"N, 7°37'2"W
Telephone: +34 6 4564 9496
Email: info@afontanadeluxo.com
Web: afontanadeluxo.com
Min Cost= €14, No of Beds = 18, Facilities= KITCHEN, WASHING MACHINE, TUMBLE DRYER, BICYCLE STORAGE, INTERNET
Opening Times: 12:00 till 19:30 January 1 till December 31
Booking.com: www.booking.com/hotel/es/a-fontana-de-luxo.es.html

## Albergue Pons Minea

Address: Avenida de Sarria, 11
GPS Coordinates: 42.80591, -7.61707 / 42°48'21"N, 7°37'1"W
Telephone: +34 6 1073 7995 OR +34 6 8645 6931
Email: info@ponsminea.es
Web: ponsminea.es
Min Cost= €10, No of Beds = 24, Facilities= KITCHEN, WASHING MACHINE, TUMBLE DRYER, BICYCLE STORAGE, INTERNET, PRIVATE ROOMS AVAILABLE
Opening Times: 12:00 till 19:30 January 1 till December 31
Booking.com: www.booking.com/hotel/es/pons-minea.es.html

The entrance arch (below) is made from one of the arches of the original bridge and is one of my favourite sites as it gives you the feeling of arriving.

# Chapter 5 - Portomarín to Palas de Rei

| | | | | | | | Waypoint Portomarín to Palas de Rei | | | |
|---|---|---|---|---|---|---|---|---|---|---|
| From | Waypoint | Decimal GPS | DMS GPS | Distance | 3.9 km/hr | 3.9 km/hr + breaks | 4.6 km/hr | 4.6 km/hr + breaks | 5.3 km/hr | 5.3 km/hr + breaks |
| Portomarín | Gonzar | 42.82651 -7.69629 | 42°49'35"N 7°41'47"W | 7.7km | 2hrs 30mins | 3hrs 0mins | 2hrs 7mins | 2hrs 33mins | 1hrs 50mins | 2hrs 12mins |
| Gonzar | Castromaior | 42.83173 -7.70877 | 42°49'54"N 7°42'32"W | 1.1km | 0hrs 22mins | 0hrs 27mins | 0hrs 19mins | 0hrs 23mins | 0hrs 16mins | 0hrs 19mins |
| Castromaior | Hospital da Cruz | 42.84081 -7.73411 | 42°50'27"N 7°44'3"W | 2.5km | 0hrs 48mins | 0hrs 58mins | 0hrs 41mins | 0hrs 49mins | 0hrs 35mins | 0hrs 43mins |
| Hospital da Cruz | Ventas de Narón | 42.84412 -7.74881 | 42°50'39"N 7°44'56"W | 1.5km | 0hrs 27mins | 0hrs 32mins | 0hrs 23mins | 0hrs 27mins | 0hrs 20mins | 0hrs 24mins |
| Ventas de Narón | Alto de Ligonde | 42.84847 -7.75871 | 42°50'54"N 7°45'31"W | 0.9km | 0hrs 17mins | 0hrs 21mins | 0hrs 14mins | 0hrs 17mins | 0hrs 12mins | 0hrs 15mins |
| Alto de Ligonde | Ligonde | 42.85897 -7.77990 | 42°51'32"N 7°46'48"W | 2.0km | 0hrs 33mins | 0hrs 40mins | 0hrs 28mins | 0hrs 34mins | 0hrs 24mins | 0hrs 29mins |
| Ligonde | Airexe | 42.86531 -7.78714 | 42°51'55"N 7°47'14"W | 0.9km | 5hrs 16mins | 6hrs 20mins | 4hrs 28mins | 5hrs 22mins | 3hrs 53mins | 4hrs 39mins |
| Airexe | Portos | 42.87355 -7.80710 | 42°52'25"N 7°48'26"W | 1.8km | 0hrs 33mins | 0hrs 40mins | 0hrs 28mins | 0hrs 34mins | 0hrs 24mins | 0hrs 29mins |
| Portos | Lestedo | 42.87218 -7.81411 | 42°52'20"N 7°48'51"W | 0.7km | 0hrs 14mins | 0hrs 17mins | 0hrs 12mins | 0hrs 14mins | 0hrs 10mins | 0hrs 12mins |
| Lestedo | A Brea | 42.87586 -7.83606 | 42°52'33"N 7°50'10"W | 2.0km | 0hrs 36mins | 0hrs 43mins | 0hrs 30mins | 0hrs 37mins | 0hrs 26mins | 0hrs 32mins |
| A Brea | Os Chacotes | 42.87392 -7.85711 | 42°52'26"N 7°51'26"W | 1.9km | 0hrs 33mins | 0hrs 39mins | 0hrs 28mins | 0hrs 33mins | 0hrs 24mins | 0hrs 29mins |
| Os Chacotes | Palas de Rei | 42.87278 -7.86843 | 42°52'22"N 7°52'6"W | 1.0km | 0hrs 16mins | 0hrs 20mins | 0hrs 14mins | 0hrs 17mins | 0hrs 12mins | 0hrs 14mins |
| Portomarín | Palas de Rei | 42.87278 -7.86843 | 42°52'22"N 7°52'6"W | 24.1km | 7hrs 31mins | 9hrs 1mins | 6hrs 22mins | 7hrs 39mins | 5hrs 32mins | 6hrs 38mins |

# Portomarín to Palas de Rei Elevation Chart

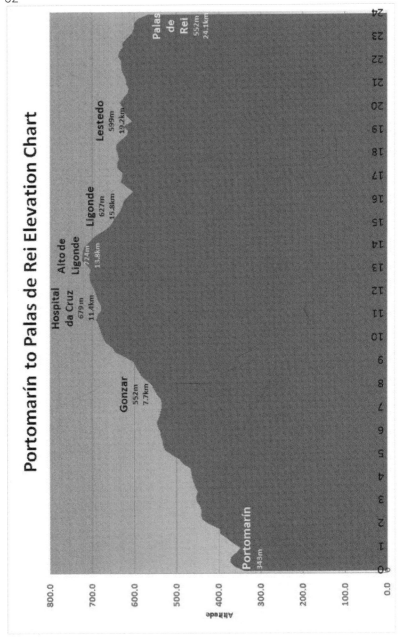

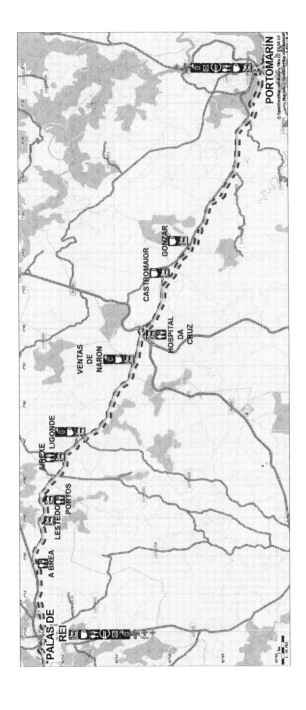

## Notes about Today's Stage

Your second day starts with a short but steep descent to re-join the Camino at the entrance of Portomarín. You then cross another part of the dam before starting today's main ascent. This ascent is about 450 metres over 9 km which is moderately demanding but is generally well shaded. The first opportunity for a break comes at about the 8km mark and three quarters up the climb in Gonzar. The next opportunity for a break comes another 1 or 2km further in Castromaior. Another 3km further is Hospital da Cruz and by this point although there is a small amount of moderate climbing left, you have completed the main ascent and it is here or in Ventas de Narón that most people choose to have their lunch break. Shortly after Hospital da Cruz you will pass through Ventas de Narón just before reaching the peak of today's walk at Alto de Ligonde (724 metres). After Alto de Ligonde, the countryside is best described as rolling, descending down through Ligonde and your last opportunity for a break today in Lestedo. Although 4km longer than yesterday and with a big climb today does not have the sharp descents which slowed you down yesterday. In total today's walk should take you about 7 and a half hours plus breaks.

# Gonzar

84km to Santiago. 1.1km to Castromayor. Altitude 551m. Available Beds=70. Local Facilities= CAFE/BAR. GPS: <u>42.826465, -7.696393</u>

# Gonzar Village Map

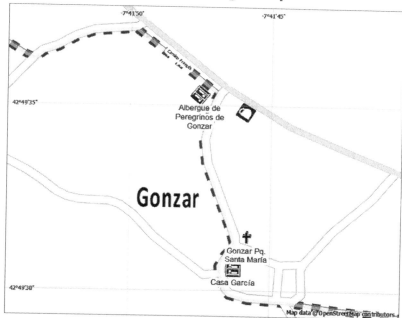

## Pilgrim Accommodation Gonzar

### Albergue Xunta

Address: Beside the road
GPS Coordinates: 42.82639, -7.69613 / 42°49'35"N, 7°41'46"W
Telephone: +34 9 8215 7840
Web: camino.xacobeo.es/albergues/albergue-de-gonzar
Min Cost= €6, No of Beds = 30, Facilities= WASHING MACHINE, TUMBLE DRYER
Opening Times: 13:00 till 23:00 January 1 till December 31

### Albergue Casa Garcia

Address: Gonzar, 3
GPS Coordinates: 42.82515, -7.69621 / 42°49'31"N, 7°41'46"W
Telephone: +34 9 8215 7842 OR +34 6 7086 2386
Min Cost= €10, No of Beds = 40, Facilities= WASHING MACHINE, TUMBLE DRYER, BICYCLE STORAGE, PRIVATE ROOMS AVAILABLE
Opening Times: 12:00 till 23:00 Holy Week till November 30

## Notes on Gonzar

The hike up to Gonzar is a long and demanding hike mostly through woods but with big chunks by the roadside. Just before you reach Gonzar you have the choice of following the Camino through the village or staying on the main road. Whilst I would normally advocate the few hundred extra metres for a gentle stroll through the village, at this point I think most people need a break and I would advise going with the road route up to the cafe which is nearby. The cafe on the roadside next door to the albergue does very good hot plates of food but is often very busy. If it is too busy, Albergue Ortiz is less than a kilometre away and has a café. Additionally, there is another small cafe in Castromaior just over a kilometre away.

# Castromaior

83km to Santiago. 2.5km to Hospital da Cruz. Altitude 601m. Available Beds=18. Local Facilities= CAFE/BAR, HOTEL OR GUEST HOUSE TYPE ACCOMMODATION. GPS: 42.831738, -7.708704

## Pilgrim Accommodation Castromaior

### Albergue Ortiz

Address: Castromaior, 2
GPS Coordinates: 42.83058, -7.70432 / 42°49'50"N, 7°42'16"W
Telephone: +34 9 8209 9416
Email: info@albergueortiz.com
Web: albergueortiz.com
Min Cost= €10, No of Beds = 18, Facilities= WASHING MACHINE, TUMBLE DRYER, BICYCLE STORAGE, INTERNET
Opening Times: 10:00 till 22:30 March 1 till November 30

## Notes on Castromaior

Castromaior gets its name from the original Celtic hill fort (castro) and there has been an archaeological excavation of this original iron age settlement (which dates from the second century BC to the first century AD). This archaeological excavation is in the area to your left just after you leave Castromaior itself. Please note that the local authorities are not keen to promote the site in case an influx of visitors damages the site. What is worth visiting in Castromaior is the small but well preserved 12th century Romanesque church of Santa María de Castromaior which has a wooden Romanesque statue of the Virgin as well as a Baroque retablo.

# Hospital da Cruz

81km to Santiago. 1.5km to Ventas de Narón. Altitude 679m.
Available Beds=32. Local Facilities= RESTAURANT. GPS: <u>42.840777,</u>
<u>-7.73409</u>

## Hospital da Cruz Village Map

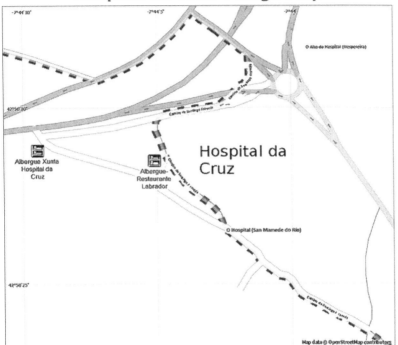

## Pilgrim Accommodation Hospital da Cruz

### Albergue Xunta

Address: O Hospital, s/n San Mamede do Río
GPS Coordinates: <u>42.84078, -7.73405</u> / 42°50'27"N, 7°44'3"W
Telephone: <u>+34 9 8254 5232</u>
Web: <u>camino.xacobeo.es/albergues/albergue-de-hospital-da-cruz</u>
Min Cost= €6, No of Beds = 32, Facilities= KITCHEN, WASHING
MACHINE, TUMBLE DRYER
Opening Times: 13:00 till 23:00 January 1 till December 31

# Ventas de Narón

79km to Santiago. 0.9km to Ligonde. Altitude 702m. Available
Beds=44. Local Facilities= CAFE/BAR. GPS: <u>42.84425, -7.74888</u>

## Notes on Ventas de Narón

In medieval times, the town was known as Sala Regine and is mentioned in the Codex Calixtinus. Its current name Ventas (meaning sales) possibly indicates that it was once a place of trade on the Camino. It had a pilgrim hostel built in the 13th century by the Knights Templar of which the only remaining part is the Capilla de Santa María Magdalena on the outskirts of the hamlet. If you wish to access to this chapel there is a phone number on the door you can ring and somebody from the village will come and open it for you. The village was also the site of a battle in 820 to defeat the invading forces of the Emir of Córdoba. Now it is nothing more than a peaceful hamlet that provides an excellent opportunity for lunch.

## Ventas de Narón Village Map

Map data © OpenStreetMap contributors

## Pilgrim Accommodation Ventas de Narón

### Albergue Casa Molar

Address: Ventas de Narón, 4
GPS Coordinates: 42.84422, -7.74776 / 42°50'39"N, 7°44'52"W
Telephone: +34 6 9679 4507
Email: casamolar_ventas@yahoo.es
Min Cost= €10, No of Beds = 22, Facilities= WASHING MACHINE, TUMBLE DRYER, BICYCLE STORAGE, INTERNET
Opening Times: 11:00 till 23:00 March 1 till November 30

## Albergue O Cruceiro

Address: Ventas de Narón, 6
GPS Coordinates: <u>42.84398, -7.74921</u> / 42°50'38"N, 7°44'57"W
Telephone: <u>+34 6 5806 4917</u>
Email: <u>albergueocruceiro@gmail.com</u>
Web: <u>www.albergueocruceiro.blogspot.com</u>
Min Cost= €10, No of Beds = 22, Facilities= WASHING MACHINE,
TUMBLE DRYER, BICYCLE STORAGE, INTERNET
Opening Times: 12:00 till 23:00 March 1 till December 31

# Ligonde

78km to Santiago. 2.9km to Airexe. Altitude 628m. Available
Beds=30. Local Facilities= CAFE/BAR. GPS: <u>42.858895, -7.779868</u>

## Notes on Ligonde

About 300 metres (42.85523, -7.77739) before you reach Ligonde
you come across the Cruceiro de Ligonde (the stone cross of Ligonde).
This dates from 1670 and is one of the best known Cruceiros on the
whole Camino Francés. On one side can be seen the image of the
Virgin with Christ in her arms and on the other side you can see Christ
on the cross and at the foot of Christ a skull.

Ligonde was the home of a pilgrim hospital from 956 till 1753
together with a pilgrim cemetery. All that remains today of the
cemetery is a simple cross on a stone wall.

The Albergue Fuente del Peregrino in Ligonde often offers
donativo tea, coffee, water and fruit. On a hot day this is welcome
refreshment but I normally prefer to take an extended break at Casa
Mariluz which is about  another 500m further.

## Ligonde Village Map

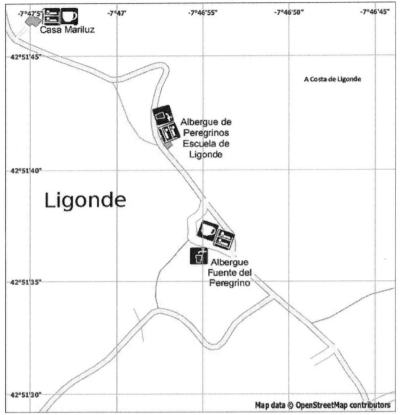

# Pilgrim Accommodation Ligonde

## Albergue Municipal Escuela de Ligonde

Address: Ligonde, s/n
GPS Coordinates: 42.86143, -7.78256 / 42°51'41"N, 7°46'57"W
Telephone: +34 6 7981 6061
Web: camino.xacobeo.es/albergues/albergue-escuela-de-ligonde
Min Cost= €8, No of Beds = 20, Facilities= KITCHEN, WASHING
MACHINE, TUMBLE DRYER, BICYCLE STORAGE, INTERNET
Opening Times: 13:00 till 23:00 January 1 till December 31

## Albergue Fuente del Peregrino

Address: Ligonde, 4
GPS Coordinates: 42.86011, -7.78153 / 42°51'36"N, 7°46'54"W

Telephone: +34 6 8755 0527
Web: lafuentedelperegrino.com/en
Min Cost= €Don., No of Beds = 10, Facilities= COMMUNAL MEAL
Opening Times: 13:00 till 22:00 April 1 till October 31

# Airexe/Eirexe

75km to Santiago. 1.8km to Portos. Altitude 632m. Available
Beds=24. Local Facilities= RESTAURANT, HOTEL OR GUEST HOUSE
TYPE ACCOMMODATION. GPS: 42.865405, -7.787265

## Notes on Airexe/Eirexe

To clear the confusion, Airexe is the Galician name for this village
and Eirexe is the Castilian (Spanish) name for this village. Of note is the
small 13th century Iglesia de Santiago.

## Airexe/Eirexe Village Map

Map data © OpenStreetMap contributors

# Pilgrim Accommodation Airexe/Eirexe

## Pensión Eirexe

GPS Coordinates: <u>42.86574, -7.78719</u> / 42°51'57"N, 7°47'14"W
Telephone: <u>+34 9 8215 3475</u> OR <u>+34 6 5096 5873</u>
Email: <u>pensioneirexe@yahoo.es</u>
Min Cost= €10, No of Beds = 4, Facilities= PRIVATE ROOMS
AVAILABLE
Opening Times: 12:00 till 23:00 January 1 till December 31

## Albergue Xunta

Address: Ligonde, s/n Monterroso
GPS Coordinates: <u>42.865421, -7.78708</u> / 42°51'56"N, 7°47'13"W
Telephone: <u>+34 9 8215 3483</u>
Web: <u>camino.xacobeo.es/albergues/albergue-de-ligonde</u>
Min Cost= €6, No of Beds = 20, Facilities= KITCHEN, WASHING
MACHINE, TUMBLE DRYER, BICYCLE STORAGE
Opening Times: 13:00 till 23:00 January 1 till December 31

# Portos

74km to Santiago. 0.7km to Lestedo. Altitude 583m. Available
Beds=22. Local Facilities= RESTAURANT. GPS: <u>42.873548, -7.807055</u>

## Notes on Portos/Lestedo

The enormous ant statues in O Paso da Formiga (which translates
as the passage of the ants) are strange but amazing and the Spanish
omelette is pretty good too! Portos makes for a good afternoon stop.

## Portos/Lestedo Village Map

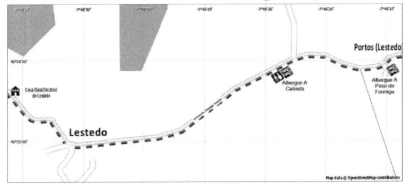

# Pilgrim Accommodation Portos

## Albergue A Calzada
GPS Coordinates: <u>42.87351, -7.80925</u> / 42°52'25"N, 7°48'33"W
Telephone: <u>+34 9 8218 3744</u>
Min Cost= €10, No of Beds = 10, Facilities= BICYCLE STORAGE
Opening Times: 12:00 till 23:00 Holy Week till September 30

## Albergue A Paso do Formiga
Address: Portos nº4. Lestedo
GPS Coordinates: <u>42.87349, -7.80706</u> / 42°52'25"N, 7°48'25"W
Telephone: <u>+34 6 1898 4605</u>
Email: <u>apasodeformiga@hotmail.com</u>
Web: <u>apasodeformiga.com</u>
Min Cost= €10, No of Beds = 12, Facilities= WASHING MACHINE,
TUMBLE DRYER, BICYCLE STORAGE, INTERNET, PRIVATE ROOMS
AVAILABLE
Opening Times: 10:00 till 22:00 Holy Week till October 31

# Lestedo
73km to Santiago. 2km to A Brea. Altitude 599m. Local Facilities=
HOTEL OR GUEST HOUSE TYPE ACCOMMODATION. GPS: <u>42.872183,
-7.814183</u>

# A Brea
71km to Santiago. 1.9km to Os Chacotes. Altitude 621m. Local
Facilities= CAFE/BAR, RESTAURANT. GPS: <u>42.87589, -7.83604</u>

# Os Chacotes
69km to Santiago. 1km to Palas de Rei. Altitude 609m. Available
Beds=112. Local Facilities= RESTAURANT. GPS: <u>42.87392322, -
7.857112717</u>

## Notes on Os Chacotes
If you prefer staying in the countryside rather than the town then
this may be for you. However, its modern but basic style is not for me.
For me Os Chacotes has the feel of a sports resort rather than a
pilgrim's hostel and it is 1km to the nearest shops or restaurants in
Palas de Rei itself.

## Os Chacotes Village Map

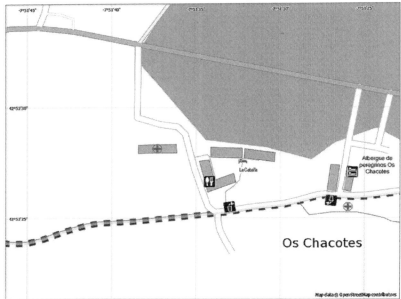

## Pilgrim Accommodation Os Chacotes

### Albergue Xunta

Address: Lugar de Chacotes, s/n
GPS Coordinates: <u>42.874076, -7.857182</u> / 42°52'27"N, 7°51'26"W
Telephone: <u>+34 6 0748 1536</u>
Web: <u>camino.xacobeo.es/albergues/albergue-de-os-chacotes</u>
Min Cost= €6, No of Beds = 112, Facilities= KITCHEN, WASHING
MACHINE, TUMBLE DRYER, BICYCLE STORAGE
Opening Times: 13:00 till 22:00 January 1 till December 31

# Palas de Rei

68km to Santiago. 3.5km to San Xulián do Camiño. Altitude
554m. Available Beds=435. Local Facilities= CAFE/BAR,
RESTAURANT, ATM, HOTEL OR GUEST HOUSE TYPE
ACCOMMODATION, PHARMACY, MEDICAL CENTRE, GROCERY
STORE. GPS: <u>42.873211, -7.869131</u>

### Notes on Palas de Rei

Palas de Rei has been a traditional overnight stay for pilgrims
since the times of the Codex Calixtinus. Its name which means palace
of the king relates to the palace built by the Visigoth king Witiza (702

to 710). There are no remains of this palace and the oldest historic surviving building is the 12th century Romanesque Iglesia de San Tirso. This is the church which you walk right past on the Camino on your way into Palas de Rei. In terms of stamps, San Tirso claims the second oldest stamp on the Camino, only second in age to the final stamp at the pilgrim's office in Santiago. It also forms a meeting point for those without rooms when all accommodation is fully booked. If all accommodation is fully booked often the local councils will open up school buildings to house homeless pilgrims for the night. Whilst I personally dislike the loss of freedom by booking ahead, none the less at peak times it is advised to book your accommodation a couple of days in advance and for the Sarria to Santiago pilgrimage it is advised to book all your accommodation when you book your travel. Whilst on the subject of good advice, I have heard some pilgrims say that the Galicians are not very welcoming; I have to say that my experience has been the complete opposite and my advice concerning Galician hospitality is that when your host suggests moving on to the local Aguardente liquor called Orujo it is time to remember that you are on a pilgrimage and it is definitely time for bed! Excess of Galician hospitality does not make for a great day's walking the following day!

When leaving Palas de Rei in the morning there are not many cafe/bars open for breakfast except for the cafe/bar Britania opposite the municipal albergue Xunta. Also, when leaving take a moment to look over the very pretty flowerbed made into the coat of arms of Palas de Rei.

# Palas de Rei Town Map

A Albergue A Casina di Marcello
B Albergue Buen Camino
C Albergue Xunta de Palas de Rei
D Albergue Castro
E Albergue San Marcos
F Pensión O'Cruceiro
G Hostel O Castelo
H Albergue Mesón de Benito
I Albergue Zendoira

## Pilgrim Accommodation Palas do Rei

### Albergue Xunta

Address: Avenida de Compostela, 19
GPS Coordinates: 42.87316, -7.86902 / 42°52'23"N, 7°52'8"W
Telephone: +34 6 6039 6820
Web: camino.xacobeo.es/albergues/albergue-de-palas-de-rei
Min Cost= €6, No of Beds = 60, Facilities= KITCHEN, WASHING
MACHINE, TUMBLE DRYER, BICYCLE STORAGE,#
Opening Times: 13:00 till 23:00 January 1 till December 31

### Albergue Mesón de Benito

Address: Rúa da Paz, S/N
GPS Coordinates: 42.87223, -7.86742 / 42°52'20"N, 7°52'3"W

Telephone: +34 6 3683 4065 OR +34 6 6723 2184
Email: info@alberguemesondebenito.com
Web: alberguemesondebenito.com
Min Cost= €10, No of Beds = 100, Facilities= WASHING MACHINE,
TUMBLE DRYER, BICYCLE STORAGE, INTERNET
Opening Times: 12:00 till 00:00 Holy Week till October 31

## Albergue San Marcos

Address: Travesía da Igrexa, 2
GPS Coordinates: 42.87258, -7.86818 / 42°52'21"N, 7°52'5"W
Telephone: +34 9 8238 0711
Email: info@alberguesanmarcos.es
Web: alberguesanmarcos.com
Min Cost= €10, No of Beds = 71, Facilities= KITCHEN, WASHING
MACHINE, TUMBLE DRYER, BICYCLE STORAGE, INTERNET
Opening Times: 11:00 till 23:00 March 1 till November 30

## Albergue Outeiro

Address: Plaza de Galicia, 25
GPS Coordinates: 42.87386, -7.86744 / 42°52'26"N, 7°52'3"W
Telephone: +34 9 8238 0242 OR +34 6 3013 4357
Email: info@albergueouteiro.com
Web: www.albergueouteiro.com/en/
Min Cost= €10, No of Beds = 50, Facilities= KITCHEN, WASHING
MACHINE, TUMBLE DRYER, BICYCLE STORAGE, INTERNET
Opening Times: 11:00 till 23:00 March 1 till October 31
Booking.com: www.booking.com/hotel/es/albergue-outeiro.en-
gb.html

## Albergue Zendoira

Address: Rúa Amado Losada 10
GPS Coordinates: 42.86905, -7.86826 / 42°52'9"N, 7°52'6"W
Telephone: +34 6 0849 0075
Email: info@zendoira.com
Web: zendoira.com
Min Cost= €10, No of Beds = 50, Facilities= KITCHEN, WASHING
MACHINE, TUMBLE DRYER, BICYCLE STORAGE, INTERNET, PRIVATE
ROOMS AVAILABLE
Opening Times: 10:00 till N/A March 1 till October 31
Booking.com: www.booking.com/hotel/es/zendoira.en-gb.html

## Albergue Castro

Address: Avenida de Ourense, 24
GPS Coordinates: 42.87297, -7.86843 / 42°52'23"N, 7°52'6"W
Telephone: +34 9 8238 0152 OR +34 6 0908 0655

Email: info@alberguecastro.com
Web: alberguecastro.com
Min Cost= €10, No of Beds = 46, Facilities= WASHING MACHINE, TUMBLE DRYER, BICYCLE STORAGE
Opening Times: 10:00 till 23:00 January 1 till December 31

## Albergue Buen Camino

Address: Rúa do Peregrino, 3
GPS Coordinates: 42.87321, -7.86983 / 42°52'24"N, 7°52'11"W
Telephone: +34 9 8238 0233 OR +34 6 3988 2229
Email: alberguebuencamino@yahoo.es
Web: www.alberguebuencamino.com
Min Cost= €10, No of Beds = 41, Facilities= WASHING MACHINE, TUMBLE DRYER
Opening Times: 12:00 till 23:00 Holy Week till October 31

## Albergue A Casiña di Marcello

Address: Calle Camiño de abaixo
GPS Coordinates: 42.87328, -7.87267 / 42°52'24"N, 7°52'22"W
Telephone: +34 6 4072 3903 OR +393402357700
Email: albergueacasina@gmail.com
Web: www.albergueacasina.com
Min Cost= €10, No of Beds = 17, Facilities= KITCHEN, WASHING MACHINE, TUMBLE DRYER, BICYCLE STORAGE, INTERNET COMMUNAL MEAL, PRIVATE ROOMS AVAILABLE
Opening Times: 14:00 till 22:00 March 1 till November 30

# Chapter 6 - Palas de Rei to Arzúa

## Waypoint Palas de Rei to Arzúa

| From | To | Decimal GPS | DMS GPS | Distance | 3.9 km/hr | 3.9 km/hr + breaks | 4.6 km/hr | 4.6 km/hr + breaks | 5.3 km/hr | 5.3 km/hr + breaks |
|---|---|---|---|---|---|---|---|---|---|---|
| Palas de Rei | San Xulián do Camiño | 42.87451 -7.90333 | 42°52'28"N 7°54'12"W | 3.5km | 1hrs 0mins | 1hrs 12mins | 0hrs 51mins | 1hrs 1mins | 0hrs 44mins | 0hrs 53mins |
| San Xulián do Camiño | Ponte Campaña | 42.87847 -7.91439 | 42°52'43"N 7°54'52"W | 1.0km | 0hrs 17mins | 0hrs 20mins | 0hrs 14mins | 0hrs 17mins | 0hrs 12mins | 0hrs 15mins |
| Ponte Campaña | Casanova | 42.87873 -7.92815 | 42°52'43"N 7°55'41"W | 1.2km | 0hrs 24mins | 0hrs 29mins | 0hrs 20mins | 0hrs 24mins | 0hrs 18mins | 0hrs 21mins |
| Casanova | Leboreiro | 42.88770 -7.96556 | 42°53'16"N 7°57'56"W | 3.3km | 1hrs 0mins | 1hrs 12mins | 0hrs 51mins | 1hrs 1mins | 0hrs 44mins | 0hrs 53mins |
| Leboreiro | Furelos | 42.90927 -7.99982 | 42°54'33"N 7°59'59"W | 3.6km | 1hrs 4mins | 1hrs 17mins | 0hrs 54mins | 1hrs 5mins | 0hrs 47mins | 0hrs 56mins |
| Furelos | Melide | 42.91406 -8.01464 | 42°54'51"N 8°0'53"W | 1.3km | 0hrs 25mins | 0hrs 30mins | 0hrs 21mins | 0hrs 25mins | 0hrs 18mins | 0hrs 22mins |
| Melide | Boente | 42.91643 -8.07801 | 42°54'59"N 8°4'41"W | 5.9km | 1hrs 46mins | 2hrs 7mins | 1hrs 30mins | 1hrs 48mins | 1hrs 18mins | 1hrs 34mins |
| Boente | Castañeda | 42.92592 -8.10414 | 42°55'33"N 8°6'15"W | 2.7km | 0hrs 49mins | 0hrs 59mins | 0hrs 41mins | 0hrs 50mins | 0hrs 36mins | 0hrs 43mins |
| Castañeda | Ribadiso da Baixo | 42.93067 -8.13069 | 42°55'50"N 8°7'50"W | 2.4km | 0hrs 43mins | 0hrs 52mins | 0hrs 37mins | 0hrs 44mins | 0hrs 32mins | 0hrs 38mins |
| Ribadiso da Baixo | Arzúa | 42.92662 -8.16248 | 42°55'36"N 8°9'45"W | 3.2km | 1hrs 1mins | 1hrs 14mins | 0hrs 52mins | 1hrs 2mins | 0hrs 45mins | 0hrs 54mins |
| Palas de Rei | Arzúa | 42.92662 -8.16248 | 42°55'36"N 8°9'45"W | 28.2km | 8hrs 34mins | 10hrs 17mins | 7hrs 16mins | 8hrs 43mins | 6hrs 18mins | 7hrs 34mins |

# Palas de to Arzúa Rei Elevation Chart

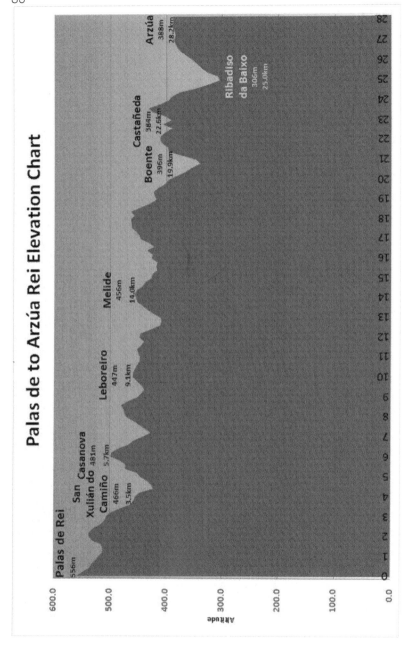

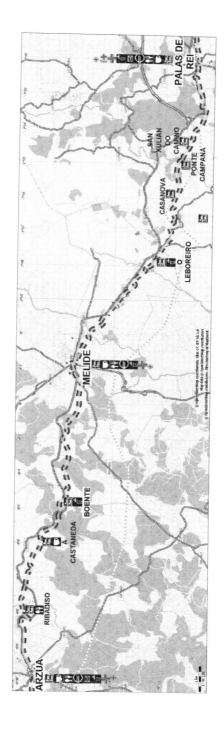

## Notes about Today's Stage

At 28k today is the most demanding of your pilgrimage and involves about 8 and a half hours of walking plus breaks. Although overall you descend over 150 metres, you are frequently going up and downhill. This is the most demanding day which many of us choose to shorten slightly by staying in Ribadiso rather than making the full way to Arzúa. Some also choose to break this day in to two days by staying overnight in Melide, which is an option if you want to make a 6 day rather than a 5 day Camino.

The highlight of today is lunch in Melide which is reputed to have the best pulpo (octopus) in the whole of Galicia. Whether this is true or not I cannot say but I can say that the pulpo is very good. If octopus is not to your taste, then the restaurants do very good spit roast chicken and steaks as well. The Camino tradition is to have pulpo in A Garnacha (on the corner as you turn on to the high street) or Ezequiels (just further down the high street on the same side). The locals rate both restaurants as equally excellent, with Ezequiels being the more traditional of the two but my personal preference is for A Garnacha. If you are unsure about eating Octopus, there is usually a good selection of other dishes including Padron peppers, French fries, steak (in A Garnacha) and chicken (in Ezequiels). In A Garnacha the cheesecake is a truly exceptional dessert but remember you still have a long walk in the afternoon. There are plenty of opportunities for breaks every 4 or 5 kilometres today and I am a great believer that much of the magic of the Camino is worked when you sit down and share a drink and chat with people you have previously only said "buen camino" to along the way.

# San Xulián do Camiño

65km to Santiago. 1km to Ponte Campaña. Altitude 467m. Available Beds=12. Local Facilities= NONE. GPS: <u>42.874436, -7.903214</u>

## Notes on San Xulián do Camiño

The story of Saint Julian the Hospitaller is a strange but apt story for the Camino in that Saint Julian uses pilgrimage and hospitality to pilgrims to atone for his terrible sin of killing his parents. Before telling the story it is worth noting that Saint Julian is the patron saint of the following: boatmen, carnival workers, childless people, circus workers, clowns, ferrymen, fiddle players, hospitallers, hotel-keepers, hunters, innkeepers, jugglers, wandering musicians, knights, murderers, pilgrims, shepherds, travellers and, in of particular interest to us pilgrims, to obtain lodging while traveling.

The story of Saint Julian starts with the night of his birth in Le Mans, France when his father witnessed pagan witches curse his son into killing both his parents. His father wanted to get rid of the child, but his mother would not let him do so. As Julian grew up he found out about the curse (some legends tell that he was told of the curse by a stag while out hunting). Julian decided he would prevent the curse from ever happening by leaving home and moving far away. After walking 50 days Julian reached Galicia and settled down with a good wife. Some twenty years later his parents made a pilgrimage to Santiago. While Julian was out hunting, Julian's wife not knowing his parents put up the two tired old pilgrims in her own bed. Upon his return, Julian came across the couple in his marital bed and believing them to be his wife with a lover he murdered both them in a fit of rage. When he realised his mistake, Julian was horrified by what he had done but his wife consoled him and told him to trust in Christ's forgiveness and persuaded him to atone by making a pilgrimage to Rome. After this pilgrimage, Saint Julian set up several pilgrim hostels and dedicated his life to caring for pilgrims on their pilgrimage and in this way gradually atoned for his terrible sin.

## San Xulián do Camiño Village Map

# Pilgrim Accommodation San Xulián do Camiño

## Albergue O Abrigadoiro

GPS Coordinates: <u>42.87447, -7.9035</u> / 42°52'28"N, 7°54'13"W
Telephone: <u>+34 6 7659 6975</u>
Email: <u>medeagomez@yahoo.es</u>
Web: <u>abrigadoiro.es.tl</u>
Min Cost= €12, No of Beds = 12, Facilities= WASHING MACHINE, TUMBLE DRYER, BICYCLE STORAGE, INTERNET, COMMUNAL MEAL
Opening Times: 12:00 till 23:00 Holy Week till October 31

# Ponte Campaña

64km to Santiago. 1.2km to Casanova. Altitude 422m. Available Beds=18. Local Facilities= NONE. GPS: <u>42.878383, -7.914399</u>

## Notes on Ponte Campaña

Watch out for the huge shell on the Albergue Casa Domingo just after you pass the small bridge over the Río Pambre.

## Ponte Campaña Village Map

## Pilgrim Accommodation Ponte Campaña

### Albergue Casa Domingo

GPS Coordinates: <u>42.87807, -7.91453</u> / 42°52'41"N, 7°54'52"W
Telephone: <u>+34 9 8216 3226</u> OR <u>+34 6 3072 8864</u>
Email: <u>info@alberguecasadomingo.com</u>
Web: <u>www.alberguecasadomingo.com</u>
Min Cost= €10, No of Beds = 18, Facilities= WASHING MACHINE, TUMBLE DRYER, BICYCLE STORAGE, INTERNET, COMMUNAL MEAL

Opening Times: 12:00 till 23:00 Holy Week till October 31

# Casanova

62km to Santiago. 3.3km to Leboreiro. Altitude 482m. Available Beds=42. Local Facilities= NONE. GPS: 42.878733, -7.928281

## Notes on Casanova

There are two cafes in Casanova next to each other. Most pilgrims stop in the first café which has good empanadas but personally I would recommend the Taberna Casanova next door as it has the best Spanish Omelette I have ever tasted.

Please note that the Albergue A Bolboreta will generally pick you up, if you fancy staying there but resent the extra distance off-Camino you would have to walk.

## Casanova Village Map

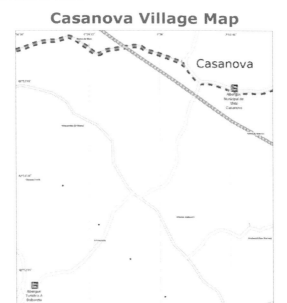

## Pilgrim Accommodation Casanova

### Albergue Xunta

Address: Santiago, 61
GPS Coordinates: 42.878834, -7.928939 / 42°52'44"N, 7°55'44"W
Telephone: +34 9 8217 3483
Web: camino.xacobeo.es/albergues/albergue-de-o-mato
Min Cost= €6, No of Beds = 20, Facilities= KITCHEN, WASHING MACHINE, TUMBLE DRYER

Opening Times: 13:00 till 23:00 January 1 till December 31

## Albergue A Bolboreta

GPS Coordinates: <u>42.87024, -7.94072</u> / 42°52'13"N, 7°56'27"W
Telephone: <u>+34 6 0912 4717</u>
Email: <u>montse@abolboreta.com</u>
Web: <u>www.abolboreta.com</u>
Min Cost= €13, No of Beds = 22, Facilities= WASHING MACHINE, TUMBLE DRYER, BICYCLE STORAGE, INTERNET, COMMUNAL MEAL, PRIVATE ROOMS AVAILABLE
Opening Times: 12:00 till N/A January 7 till December 23
Booking.com: <u>www.booking.com/hotel/es/a-bolboreta.en-gb.html</u>

# Leboreiro

59km to Santiago. 3.6km to Furelos. Altitude 447m. Local Facilities= HOTEL OR GUEST HOUSE TYPE ACCOMMODATION. GPS: <u>42.887994, -7.965597</u>

## Notes on Leboreiro

Leboreiro is also mentioned in the Codex Calixtinus but not in subsequent guides and we can only assume its importance diminished. Of note in Leboreiro is the 13th century gothic church of Santa María de Leboreiro which although technically Gothic has several Romanesque features. On the outside above the entrance is a beautiful engraving of the Virgin and Child (this type of image above the entrance to a church is called a tympanum). There is a legend associated with this engraving. The legend goes that the villages noticed a strange light and a beautiful fragrance coming from a nearby fountain. Suspecting a miracle, the villagers started digging around the fountain and uncovered an image of the Virgin. They took the image back to the church and placed it on the altar. However, the Virgin was not happy with this and the image returned to the fountain at night. The following day the villagers reclaimed the image and bought it back to the church. This transporting of the image of the Virgin carried on for a few days until a local sculptor had the idea of sculpting an image of the Virgin on the tympanum and rededicating the church to the Virgin. After which the image of the Virgin was happy to remain in the church. Inside the church is a 14th century statue of the Virgin and a 16th century painted mural which depicts the visitation of Saint Elizabeth to the Virgin, the flagellation of Christ and the martyrdom of San Sebastián.

# Furelos

55km to Santiago. 1.3km to Melide. Altitude 409m. Local Facilities=
NONE. GPS: 42.909259, -7.999944

## Notes on Furelos

This village was once run by the Order of Knights of the Hospital
of Saint John of Jerusalem (whose emblem is a Maltese Cross). They
are also known as the Knights Hospitaller and had a dual role of caring
for the sick and the protection of pilgrims. There is little left of the
pilgrim hospital they once ran here and even the 13th century church
of San Juan has been heavily remodelled in the 1920s in a neogothic
style leaving little of the original church visible. The medieval bridge,
however, is probably the best of the many bridges on the Camino
through Galicia and is one my favourite spots for taking photographs.

# Melide

54km to Santiago. 5.9km to Boente. Altitude 456m. Available
Beds=467. Local Facilities= CAFE/BAR, RESTAURANT, ATM, HOTEL
OR GUEST HOUSE TYPE ACCOMMODATION, PHARMACY, MEDICAL
CENTRE, GROCERY STORE. GPS: 42.913893, -8.014727

## Notes on Melide

There has been a settlement around Melide since Neolithic
times. In Roman times, it was the crossing point of two major
Roman roads, the Via Trajana and the road to the province of
Cantabria. But much of its growth and status in the middle ages
are owed to its position on both the Camino Francés and the
Camino Primitivo (which starts in Oviedo).

Melide is a big, busy and modern town but has several
buildings of note including the present chapel of San Pedro and
San Roque, located on the corner of San Roque, built in 1949
with materials from the two demolished medieval churches of
San Pedro and San Roque. Its beautiful entrance comes from
the old Romanesque church of San Pedro. Inside the retablo
(altarpiece) dates from the nineteenth century, with the central
image being of San Roque. Also, inside are various 14th century
tombs. Outside is one of the oldest cruceiros (stone crosses) on
the Camino which is thought to date from the 14th century. The
front depicts Christ sitting in Glory showing his wounded hands,
the rear depicts Christ's suffering on the cross.

The church of Sancti Spiritus, in the Plaza del Convento, was part of the monastery of the Third Order of St. Francis which was founded in the fourteenth century. Of this 14th century church all that remains is a small side chapel. In 1498, Sancho Sanchez de Ulloa decided to rebuild the convent church in memory of his mother Ines de Castro using the stone from the remains of the castle.

There is daily mass at 17:30h (except in July and August when mass is at 18:00h) in the Capilla del Carmen on the way out of Melide along the Camino in Rúa Principal. This chapel was built in 1741, on the site where the medieval castle of Melide had once stood.

My favourite church in Melide is the 12th century Romanesque Iglesia de Santa Maria which is about 5 minutes out of town just by what used to be the 50km marker (which is now the 51.629 km marker) that is the front cover to this book. Recently, a guide has been in attendance in the afternoons to give pilgrims a guided tour of this charming chapel in return for a small donation. This chapel and its beautiful Romanesque retablo (altarpiece) is dedicated to Our Lady of the Snows.

# Melide Town Map

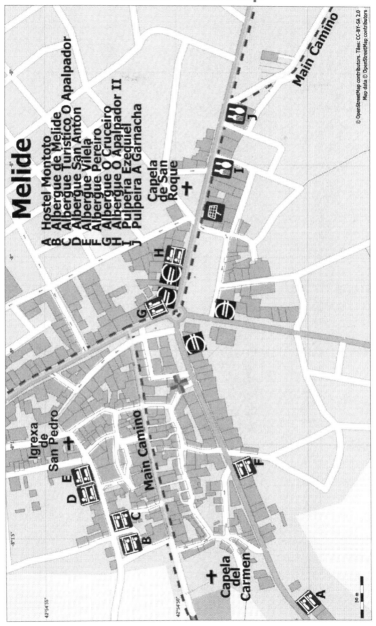

## Melide

- A Hostel Montoto
- B Albergue de Melide
- C Albergue Turístico O Apalpador
- D Albergue San Antón
- E Albergue Vilela
- F Albergue Pereiro
- G Albergue O Cruceiro
- H Albergue O Apalpador II
- I Pulpería Ezequiel
- J Pulpeira A Garnacha

Capela de San Roque

Igrexa de San Pedro

Capela del Carmen

Main Camino

# Pilgrim Accommodation Melide

## Albergue Xunta

Address: Rúa San Antonio
GPS Coordinates: 42.914471, -8.01819 / 42°54'52"N, 8°1'5"W
Telephone: +34 6 6039 6822
Web: camino.xacobeo.es/albergues/albergue-de-melide
Min Cost= €6, No of Beds = 156, Facilities= KITCHEN, WASHING
MACHINE, TUMBLE DRYER, BICYCLE STORAGE
Opening Times: 13:00 till 23:00 January 1 till December 31

## Albergue Turistico O Apalpador

Address: Rúa San Antonio, 23
GPS Coordinates: 42.91458, -8.01791 / 42°54'52"N, 8°1'4"W
Telephone: +34 9 8150 6266 OR +34 6 7983 7969
Email: info@opalpador.com
Web: www.albergueoapalpador.com
Min Cost= €10, No of Beds = 54, Facilities= KITCHEN, WASHING
MACHINE, TUMBLE DRYER, BICYCLE STORAGE, INTERNET
Opening Times: 11:00 till 23:00 January 1 till December 31

## Albergue Pereiro

Address: Rúa Progreso, 43
GPS Coordinates: 42.91315, -8.017361 / 42°54'47"N, 8°1'2"W
Telephone: +34 9 8150 6314
Email: info@alberguepereiro.com
Web: www.alberguepereiro.com
Min Cost= €10, No of Beds = 45, Facilities= KITCHEN, WASHING
MACHINE, TUMBLE DRYER, BICYCLE STORAGE, INTERNET
Opening Times: 11:00 till 23:00 January 1 till December 31
Booking.com: www.booking.com/hotel/es/hostel-pereiro.en-
gb.html

## Hostel Montoto

Address: Rúa Codeseira, 31
GPS Coordinates: 42.91252, -8.01911 / 42°54'45"N, 8°1'9"W
Telephone: +34 9 8150 7337 OR +34 6 4694 1887
Email: alberguemontoto@gmail.com
Web: www.alberguemontoto.com
Min Cost= €10, No of Beds = 42, Facilities= KITCHEN, WASHING
MACHINE, TUMBLE DRYER, BICYCLE STORAGE, INTERNET
Opening Times: 11:00 till 23:00 Holy Week till October 31
Booking.com: www.booking.com/hotel/es/albergue-
montoto.es.html

### Albergue San Anton

Address: Rúa San Antonio, 6
GPS Coordinates: 42.91475, -8.017104 / 42°54'53"N, 8°1'2"W
Telephone: +34 9 8150 6427 OR +34 6 9815 3672
Email: alberguesananton@gmail.com
Web: www.alberguesananton.com
Min Cost= €10, No of Beds = 36, Facilities= KITCHEN, WASHING MACHINE, TUMBLE DRYER, BICYCLE STORAGE, INTERNET
Opening Times: 10:30 till 23:00 March 1 till November 30
Booking.com: www.booking.com/hotel/es/albergue-san-anton.html

### Albergue Alfonso II

Address: Avenida Toques e Friol, 52
GPS Coordinates: 42.91824, -8.01469 / 42°55'6"N, 8°0'53"W
Telephone: +34 9 8150 6454 OR +34 6 0860 4850
Email: info@alberguealfonsoelcasto.com
Web: www.alberguealfonsoelcasto.com
Min Cost= €10, No of Beds = 34, Facilities= KITCHEN, WASHING MACHINE, TUMBLE DRYER, BICYCLE STORAGE, INTERNET
Opening Times: 11:30 till 23:00 March 1 till October 31
Booking.com: www.booking.com/hotel/es/albergue-alfonso-ii.html

### Albergue Vilela

Address: Rúa San Antonio, 2
GPS Coordinates: 42.91477, -8.01705 / 42°54'53"N, 8°1'1"W
Telephone: +34 6 1601 1375
Min Cost= €10, No of Beds = 28, Facilities= KITCHEN, WASHING MACHINE, TUMBLE DRYER, BICYCLE STORAGE, INTERNET
Opening Times: 11:00 till 23:00 January 1 till December 31

### Albergue O Cruceiro

Address: Ronda de A Coruña, 2
GPS Coordinates: 42.9141, -8.01471 / 42°54'51"N, 8°0'53"W
Telephone: +34 6 1676 4896
Email: albergueocruceiro@yahoo.es
Web: www.albergueocruceiro.es/index.php/en
Min Cost= €12, No of Beds = 72, Facilities= KITCHEN, WASHING MACHINE, TUMBLE DRYER, BICYCLE STORAGE, INTERNET
Opening Times: 11:00 till 23:00 Holy Week till October 31

## Boente

48km to Santiago. 2.7km to Castañeda. Altitude 396m. Available Beds=74. Local Facilities= NONE. GPS: 42.916199, -8.078012

## Notes on Boente

The church of Santiago de Boente is a 20th century church but generally is left open and provides the opportunity to get 5 minutes of calm and coolness on a sweltering day as well as a stamp.

The fountain next to the stone cross in Boente called the Fonte de Saleta is said to have curative powers. In my experience, any water fountain on a sweltering day has curative powers.

## Boente Village Map

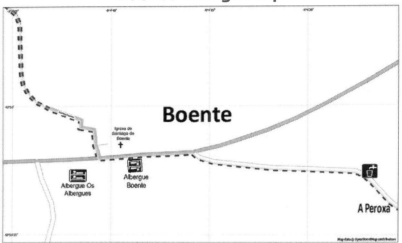

## Pilgrim Accommodation Boente

### Albergue Boente

Address: Boente – Arzúa
GPS Coordinates: 42.91608, -8.07751 / 42°54'58"N, 8°4'39"W
Telephone: +34 9 8150 1974 OR +34 6 3832 1707
Email: albergueboente@hotmail.es
Web: albergueboente.com
Min Cost= €10, No of Beds = 44, Facilities= WASHING MACHINE, TUMBLE DRYER, BICYCLE STORAGE, INTERNET, SWIMMING POOL
Opening Times: 12:00 till 23:00 March 1 till November 30

### Albergue Bar Os Albergues

Address: Boente – Arzúa
GPS Coordinates: 42.91587, -8.0782 / 42°54'57"N, 8°4'42"W
Telephone: +34 9 8150 1853
Email: os_albergues@hotmail.es

Min Cost= €10, No of Beds = 30, Facilities= WASHING MACHINE, TUMBLE DRYER, BICYCLE STORAGE, INTERNET
Opening Times: 11:00 till 23:00 March 1 till November 30

# Castañeda

46km to Santiago. 2.4km to Ribadiso da Baixo. Altitude 383m. Available Beds=6. Local Facilities= CAFE/BAR. GPS: 42.926066, -8.10416

## Notes on Castañeda

In medieval times pilgrims were asked to carry limestone from Triacastela (about 25km before Sarria) to Castañeda where it would be slaked in the ovens and used in the construction of the cathedral at Santiago.

## Castañeda Village Map

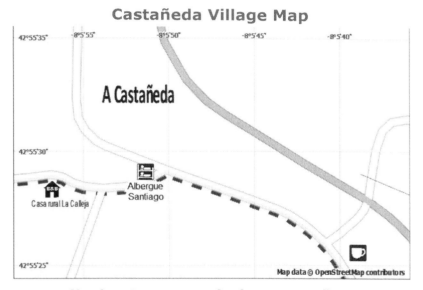

## Pilgrim Accommodation Castañeda

### Albergue Bar Santiago

Address: Castañeda
GPS Coordinates: 42.92476, -8.0974 / 42°55'29"N, 8°5'51"W
Telephone: +34 9 8150 1711 OR +34 6 9976 1698
Email: albergue.santiago.castaneda@gmail.com
Min Cost= €11, No of Beds = 6, Facilities= WASHING MACHINE, TUMBLE DRYER, BICYCLE STORAGE, INTERNET, PRIVATE ROOMS AVAILABLE
Opening Times: 12:00 till N/A January 1 till December 31

# Ribadiso da Baixo

43km to Santiago. 3.2km to Arzúa. Altitude 306m. Available Beds=158. Local Facilities= CAFE/BAR, RESTAURANT. GPS: 42.930683, -8.130634

## Notes on Ribadiso da Baixo

The municipal (Xunta) albergue in Ribadiso backs onto the river next to the bridge. On hot days the river provides a lovely opportunity to paddle and cool your feet. This municipal albergue built in 1993 is on the original site of one of the medieval pilgrim hostels. If accommodation is available, Ribadiso provides a more relaxing location to spend the night than Arzúa. Though Arzúa provides more opportunities to enjoy the great local cheese.

## Ribadiso da Baixo Village Map

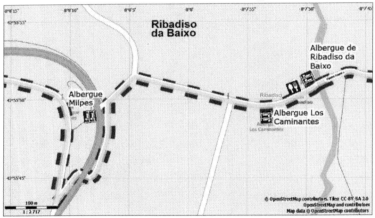

# Pilgrim Accommodation Ribadiso da Baixo

## Albergue Xunta

Address: Ribadiso de Abaixo, s/n
GPS Coordinates: 42.930872, -8.130525 / 42°55'51"N, 8°7'50"W
Telephone: +34 9 8150 1815 OR +34 6 6039 6823
Web: camino.xacobeo.es/albergues/albergue-de-ribadiso
Min Cost= €6, No of Beds = 70, Facilities= KITCHEN, WASHING
MACHINE, TUMBLE DRYER, BICYCLE STORAGE
Opening Times: 13:00 till 23:00 January 1 till December 31

### Albergue Los Caminantes

Address: Ribadiso de Abaixo, s/n
GPS Coordinates: 42.93042, -8.1314 / 42°55'50"N, 8°7'53"W
Telephone: +34 6 4702 0600
Email: info@albergueloscaminantes.com
Web: www.albergueloscaminantes.com
Min Cost= €10, No of Beds = 60, Facilities= KITCHEN, WASHING
MACHINE, TUMBLE DRYER, BICYCLE STORAGE, INTERNET
Opening Times: 12:00 till 22:30 Holy Week till October 31

### Albergue Milpes

Address: Ribadiso de Abaixo, s/n
GPS Coordinates: 42.93045, -8.13611 / 42°55'50"N, 8°8'10"W
Telephone: +34 9 8150 0425 OR +34 6 1665 2276
Email: alberguemilpes@gmail.com
Web: www.alberguemilpes.com
Min Cost= €10, No of Beds = 28, Facilities= WASHING MACHINE,
TUMBLE DRYER, BICYCLE STORAGE, INTERNET
Opening Times: 11:00 till 23:00 January 1 till December 31
Booking.com: www.booking.com/hotel/es/albergue-milpes.es.html

# Arzúa

40km to Santiago. 5.9km to Calzada. Altitude 387m. Available
Beds=481. Local Facilities= CAFE/BAR, RESTAURANT, ATM, HOTEL
OR GUEST HOUSE TYPE ACCOMMODATION, PHARMACY, MEDICAL
CENTRE, GROCERY STORE. GPS: 42.926339, -8.162618

## Notes on Arzúa

The major disadvantage of staying at Ribadiso, as I normally
choose to do, is that I pass through Arzúa early in the morning while
all the shops that sell the wonderful local cheese are still closed. As
you may have guessed I am a huge fan of the local cheese, which by
the way is excellent toasted and very good on burgers. On my bucket

list is to attend the cheese festival in Arzúa which is held the first weekend in March each year (www.festadoqueixo.org). The importance of cheese to Arzúa can also be seen in the statue in the main square which is dedicated to "La Queixeira" (the cheese maker) (42.92673, -8.16378).

In Arzúa you may be joined by pilgrims who have walked the Camino del Norte (which goes across Spain's northern coast) as the two Caminos merge.

Although the Iglesia de Santiago (42.92632, -8.16340) was re-built in the 1950s, it houses three impressive retablos (altarpieces). The main altarpiece dates from the 19th century and has at its top a depiction of Saint James intervening in the mythical battle of Clavijo. The 18th-century Rococo altarpiece of the north aisle is dedicated to Our Lady of Mount Carmel. Made in 1779 and painted in 1792 by José Edrosa the altarpiece of the Rosary located in the south aisle is the most impressive. At the centre it has an image of Our Lady of the Most Holy Rosary with Christ depicted as a child standing on a globe. The image at the top is San Roque, the patron saint invoked in times of disease or pestilence. To the left is the statue of the patron saint of farmers and labourers, Saint Isidore and to the right is the statue of Saint Raymond Nonnatus, patron saint of childbirth, midwives, children, pregnant women and priests who want to protect the secrecy of confession. Mass is said daily in the church at 19:00h.

Also of note is La Capilla de la Magdalena ( 42.92627, -8.16287) which was founded in the sixteenth century by the Augustinian Friars who created a small hospital to welcome the pilgrims. The chapel has a single rectangular nave, over the door is semi-circular arch on the facade, which reveals its Romanesque style. There are plans to turn this chapel into a small museum.

# Arzúa Town Map

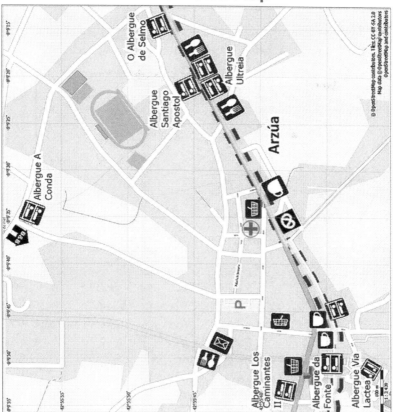

## Pilgrim Accommodation Arzúa

### Albergue Xunta

Address: Cima de Lugar, 6
GPS Coordinates: 42.926219, -8.162726 / 42°55'34"N, 8°9'46"W
Telephone: +34 6 6039 6824
Web: camino.xacobeo.es/albergues/albergue-de-arzua
Min Cost= €6, No of Beds = 50, Facilities= KITCHEN, WASHING
MACHINE, TUMBLE DRYER, BICYCLE STORAGE
Opening Times: 13:00 till 23:00 January 1 till December 31

### Albergue Via Lactea

Address: Calle José Neira Vilas, 26
GPS Coordinates: 42.92546, -8.16414 / 42°55'32"N, 8°9'51"W
Telephone: +34 9 8150 0581 OR +34 6 1675 9447

Email: vialacteaalbergue@hotmail.com

Web: www.alberguevialactea.com

Min Cost= €10, No of Beds = 60, Facilities= KITCHEN, WASHING MACHINE, TUMBLE DRYER, BICYCLE STORAGE, INTERNET

Opening Times: 12:00 till 23:00 January 1 till December 31

## Albergue Los Caminantes II

Address: Rúa de Santiago, 14

GPS Coordinates: 42.92714, -8.16511 / 42°55′38″N, 8°9′54″W

Telephone: +34 9 8150 8127 OR +34 6 4702 0600

Email: info@albergueloscaminantes.com

Web: www.albergueloscaminantes.com

Min Cost= €10, No of Beds = 60, Facilities= KITCHEN, WASHING MACHINE, TUMBLE DRYER, BICYCLE STORAGE, INTERNET

Opening Times: 11:00 till 22:30 Holy Week till October 31

## O Albergue de Selmo

Address: Rúa Lugo, 133

GPS Coordinates: 42.92976, -8.15407 / 42°55′47″N, 8°9′15″W

Telephone: +34 9 8193 9018

Email: info@oalberguedeselmo.com

Web: oalberguedeselmo.com

Min Cost= €10, No of Beds = 50, Facilities= KITCHEN, WASHING MACHINE, TUMBLE DRYER, BICYCLE STORAGE, INTERNET

Opening Times: 12:00 till 22:30 May 1 till October 31

## Albergue Don Quijote

Address: Rúa Lugo, 130

GPS Coordinates: 42.92906, -8.15538 / 42°55′45″N, 8°9′19″W

Telephone: +34 9 8150 0139 OR +34 6 9616 2695

Email: alberguedonquijote@hotmail.com

Web: www.alberguedonquijote.com

Min Cost= €10, No of Beds = 50, Facilities= KITCHEN, WASHING MACHINE, TUMBLE DRYER, BICYCLE STORAGE, INTERNET

Opening Times: 12:00 till 23:00 January 1 till December 31

## Albergue Ultreia

Address: Rúa Lugo, 126

GPS Coordinates: 42.92889, -8.15571 / 42°55′44″N, 8°9′21″W

Telephone: +34 9 8150 0471 OR +34 6 2663 9450

Email: info@albergueultreia.com

Web: www.albergueultreia.com

Min Cost= €10, No of Beds = 39, Facilities= KITCHEN, WASHING MACHINE, TUMBLE DRYER, INTERNET

Opening Times: 12:00 till 23:30 January 1 till December 31

## Albergue A Conda

Address: Rúa da Calexa, 92
GPS Coordinates: 42.93282, -8.15972 / 42°55'58"N, 8°9'35"W
Telephone: +34 9 8150 0068 OR +34 6 8792 6604
Email: hosvilarino@gmail.com
Web: www.pensionvilarino.com
Min Cost= €10, No of Beds = 18, Facilities= INTERNET
Opening Times: N/A till N/A March 1 till November 30

## Albergue Santiago Apostol

Address: Avenida de Lugo, 107
GPS Coordinates: 42.92918, -8.15556 / 42°55'45"N, 8°9'20"W
Telephone: +34 9 8150 8132 OR +34 6 6042 7771
Email: santiagoapostolalbergue@hotmail.com
Web: www.alberguesantiagoapostol.com
Min Cost= €12, No of Beds = 72, Facilities= KITCHEN, WASHING
MACHINE, TUMBLE DRYER, BICYCLE STORAGE, INTERNET
Opening Times: 12:00 till 23:00 January 1 till December 31

## Albergue da Fonte

Address: Rúa do Carmen, 18
GPS Coordinates: 42.92626, -8.16429 / 42°55'35"N, 8°9'51"W
Telephone: +34 9 8150 1118 OR +34 6 5999 9496
Email: alberguedafonte@hotmail.com
Web: www.alberguedafonte.com
Min Cost= €12, No of Beds = 20, Facilities= KITCHEN, WASHING
MACHINE, TUMBLE DRYER, INTERNET
Opening Times: 12:00 till 23:00 January 1 till December 31

## Albergue Turístico Arzúa

Address: Calle Rosalía de Castro, 2
GPS Coordinates: 42.9271, -8.16037 / 42°55'38"N, 8°9'37"W
Telephone: +34 9 8150 8233 OR +34 6 0838 0011
Email: pensionarzua@gmail.com
Min Cost= €10, No of Beds = 20, Facilities= KITCHEN, WASHING
MACHINE, TUMBLE DRYER, BICYCLE STORAGE, INTERNET
Opening Times: 12:00 till 22:00 February 1 till November 30

## De Camino Albergue

Address: Avenida de Lugo, 118
GPS Coordinates: 42.92867, -8.15616 / 42°55'43"N, 8°9'22"W
Telephone: +34 9 8150 0415
Email: info@decaminoalbergue.com
Web: www.decaminoalbergue.com

Min Cost= €10, No of Beds = 42, Facilities= WASHING MACHINE, TUMBLE DRYER, BICYCLE STORAGE, INTERNET
Opening Times: 12:00 till 22:00 February 1 till November 30

# Chapter 7 - Arzúa to Pedrouzo (Arca)

| | | | | | | | | | | |
|---|---|---|---|---|---|---|---|---|---|---|
| **Waypoints Arzúa to Pedrouzo** | | | | | | | | | | |
| From | Waypoint | Decimal GPS | DMS GPS | Distance | 3.9 km/hr | 3.9 km/hr + breaks | 4.6 km/hr | 4.6 km/hr + breaks | 5.3 km/hr | 5.3 km/hr + breaks |
| Arzúa | A Calzada | 42.92575 -8.22339 | 42°55'33"N 8°13'24"N | 5.9km | 1hrs 49mins | 2hrs 11mins | 1hrs 32mins | 1hrs 51mins | 1hrs 20mins | 1hrs 36mins |
| A Calzada | A Calle | 42.91823 -8.24335 | 42°55'6"N 8°14'36"N | 2.1km | 0hrs 36mins | 0hrs 44mins | 0hrs 31mins | 0hrs 37mins | 0hrs 27mins | 0hrs 32mins |
| A Calle | Salceda | 42.92641 -8.28033 | 42°55'35"N 8°16'49"N | 3.2km | 0hrs 59mins | 1hrs 11mins | 0hrs 50mins | 1hrs 0mins | 0hrs 43mins | 0hrs 52mins |
| Salceda | A Brea | 42.91886 -8.30530 | 42°55'8"N 8°18'19"N | 2.5km | 0hrs 46mins | 0hrs 55mins | 0hrs 39mins | 0hrs 47mins | 0hrs 34mins | 0hrs 40mins |
| A Brea | Santa Irene | 42.91831 -8.33590 | 42°55'6"N 8°20'9"N | 2.9km | 0hrs 53mins | 1hrs 4mins | 0hrs 45mins | 0hrs 54mins | 0hrs 39mins | 0hrs 47mins |
| Santa Irene | A Rua | 42.91472 -8.34965 | 42°54'53"N 8°20'59"N | 1.4km | 0hrs 23mins | 0hrs 28mins | 0hrs 19mins | 0hrs 23mins | 0hrs 17mins | 0hrs 20mins |
| A Rua | Pedrouzo | 42.90844 -8.36564 | 42°54'30"N 8°21'56"N | 2.3km | 0hrs 41mins | 0hrs 49mins | 0hrs 34mins | 0hrs 41mins | 0hrs 30mins | 0hrs 36mins |
| Arzúa | Pedrouzo | 42.90844 -8.36564 | 42°54'30"N 8°21'56"N | 20.4km | 6hrs 10mins | 7hrs 24mins | 5hrs 13mins | 6hrs 16mins | 4hrs 32mins | 5hrs 26mins |

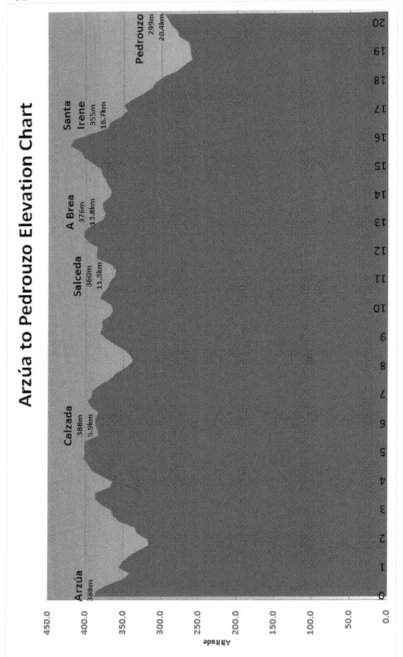

# Arzúa to Pedrouzo Elevation Chart

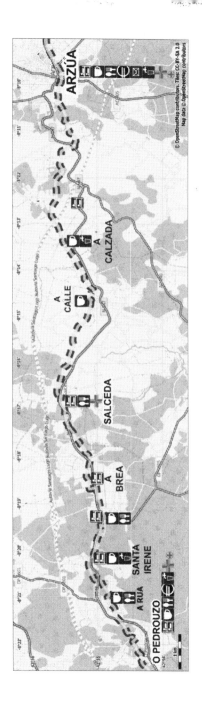

ARZÚA

A CALZADA

A CALLE

SALCEDA

A BREA

SANTA IRENE

A RUA

O PEDROUZO

1 km

## Notes about Today's Stage

Arzúa to Pedrouzo is one of my favourite days of the whole Camino. It is much less demanding than previous days and requires just over six hours of walking. Large parts of today are through wooded areas which makes for some very pleasant walking. Every 4 or 5 kilometres there are places to take a break. The scenery is lush, and many say resembles Galicia's Celtic relative Ireland. In this area it is worth trying the local Arzúa cheese which is rich and creamy because the fat content in the local milk is naturally high. It is best enjoyed with Marmelada which is quince jelly. It is hard to explain why this combination of sweet and savoury works so well, but it must be experienced to appreciate how good it is. While on the subject of food and drink, Galician beer is excellent and is enjoyed all over Northern Spain. In particular, the stronger "toasted" beers often prove to be a Camino favourite.

On the subject of beer, there is a tradition that if you stop in the cafe bar Casa Tia Teresa in the hamlet of Salceda and have a bottle of the Peregrina beer, that you should write your name, your home town and a wish on the beer bottle. The bar then displays the messages on their Facebook page and keeps the bottles to make a Christmas Tree of good wishes. The tradition originated in the bar Casa Tia Dolores in the hamlet of A Calle where the owners of Casa Tia Teresa were originally based. The new owners of Casa Tia Dolores have also adopted the tradition, so you now have at least two opportunities to enjoy a beer and make a wish.

This day is a day to enjoy and savour. With Santiago, so close at the end of today, you may be tempted to push on further. However, after Pedrouzo there are no albergues until you reach Lavacolla which is an extra 9km further or Monte do Gozo which is an extra 15km! The new albergue at Lavacolla only has limited capacity (only 34 beds) so you need to book ahead. Monte do Gozo is huge and ugly but it leaves you with only 5km to walk on the final day which makes reaching Santiago in time for the daily pilgrim mass at midday very easy. The choice is therefore between stopping at Pedrouzo and having two easy well balanced last days or going on to Lavacolla or Monte do Gozo and having a tough 30km or 35km penultimate day and extremely easy last day. If you choose to stop at Pedrouzo you will have to leave at around 6 am in order to make it in time for the pilgrim mass. Personally, I recommend Pedrouzo as I really struggle with days above 25km.

# Burres (Detour from the Camino)

35km to Santiago. Available beds=30. Local Facilities= NONE. Burres to Salceda 6.5km.

## Burres Village Map

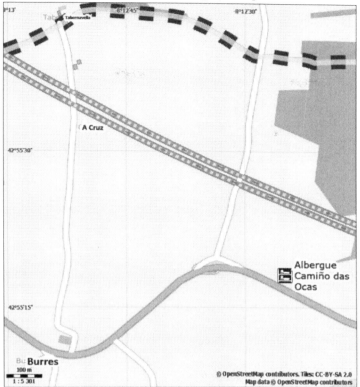

## Pilgrim Accommodation Burres

### Albergue Camino das Ocas

Address: N547 Km 68.5 Bebedeiro - Burres
GPS Coordinates: <u>42.92163, -8.20688</u> / 42°55'18"N, 8°12'25"W
Telephone: <u>+34 6 4840 4780</u>
Email: <u>contacto@caminodasocas.com</u>
Web: <u>www.caminodasocas.com</u>
Min Cost= €10, No of Beds = 30, Facilities= KITCHEN, WASHING MACHINE, TUMBLE DRYER, BICYCLE STORAGE
Opening Times: 12:00 till 22:30 March 1 till November 30

# Calzada

34km to Santiago. 2.1km to A Calle. Altitude 388m. Local Facilities= CAFE/BAR. GPS: <u>42.92575205, -8.22338705</u>

## Notes on Calzada

The cafe/bar at Calzada is just as you leave Calzada. It is a nice place to stop but it is busy, especially the queue for the ladies' toilets.

# A Calle

32km to Santiago. 3.2km to Salceda. Altitude 342m. Local Facilities= CAFE/BAR. GPS: 42.91817, -8.24333

## Notes on A Calle

The second cafe/bar in A Calle is Casa Tia Dolores where the tradition of having a beer and writing your name and a wish on the bottle originated. The new owners have carried on the tradition but be warned the new beer they use is over 7% in strength.

# Salceda

29km to Santiago. 2.5km to A Brea. Altitude 361m. Available Beds=30. Local Facilities= RESTAURANT, HOTEL OR GUEST HOUSE TYPE ACCOMMODATION, MEDICAL CENTRE. GPS: 42.9263, -8.278421

## Notes on Salceda

Salceda despite its tiny size has several albergues and bars, a restaurant, a pension and even a pharmacy. Of note is Casa Tia Teresa. The owners originally ran Café Tia Dolores in A Calle and created the Camino tradition of writing your name and your wish on a beer bottle which they then make into a Christmas tree. Unfortunately, the success of this new tradition led to an increase in rent and a forced move to a new bar in Salceda. I have enjoyed a couple of great afternoons of their hospitality and hence the shout out for their new venture here. Also of note in Salceda is the lovely garden in Meson A Esquipa.

# Salceda Town Map

## Pilgrim Accommodation Salceda

### Albergue de Boni

Address: Lugar de Salceda, 22
GPS Coordinates: 42.92654, -8.28009 / 42°55'36"N, 8°16'48"W
Telephone: +34 6 1896 5907
Email: elalberguedeboni@gmail.com
Web: elalberguedeboni.blogspot.co.uk
Min Cost= €10, No of Beds = 20, Facilities= KITCHEN, WASHING MACHINE, TUMBLE DRYER, BICYCLE STORAGE, INTERNET
Opening Times: 14:00 till 23:00 Holy Week-2 weeks - November 1

### Albergue Pousada de Salceda

Address: N-547 km75
GPS Coordinates: 42.9221, -8.27552 / 42°55'20"N, 8°16'32"W
Telephone: +34 9 8150 2767
Email: pousadadesalceda@gmail.com
Web: www.pousadadesalceda.com
Min Cost= €12, No of Beds = 10, Facilities= WASHING MACHINE, TUMBLE DRYER, BICYCLE STORAGE, INTERNET, PRIVATE ROOMS AVAILABLE
Opening Times: 12:00 till N/A January 1 till December 31
Booking.com: www.booking.com/hotel/es/complejo-turistico-salceda.es.html

### Albergue Alborada

Address: Lugar de Salceda, Ferreiros o Pino 16

GPS Coordinates: 42.92627, -8.28052 / 42°55'35"N, 8°16'50"W
Telephone: +34 6 2015 1209
Email: pensionalberguealborada@gmail.com
Web: www.facebook.com/AlbergueAlborada2016
Min Cost= €13, No of Beds = 10, Facilities= WASHING MACHINE,
TUMBLE DRYER, BICYCLE STORAGE, INTERNET, PRIVATE ROOMS
AVAILABLE
Opening Times: 12:30 till 20:00 January 1 till December 31
Booking.com: www.booking.com/hotel/es/pension-albergue-alborada.es.html

# A Brea

26km to Santiago. 2.9km to Santa Irene. Altitude 375m. Available
Beds=40. Local Facilities= CAFE/BAR. GPS: 42.918821, -8.30533

## Notes on A Brea

The albergue in A Brea is about a 400 metre detour from the
Camino.

# A Brea Village Map

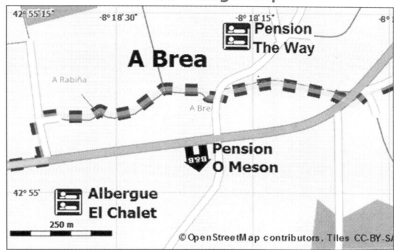

## Pilgrim Accommodation A Brea

### Albergue El Chalet
Address: Lugar A Brea, 5, O Pino (KM 24,601)
GPS Coordinates: 42.91734, -8.31049 / 42°55'2"N, 8°18'38"W
Telephone: +34 6 5938 0723
Email: elchaletalbergue@gmail.com
Web: www.facebook.com/pg/El-Chalet-Albergue-de-Peregrinos-549598555220940
Min Cost= €10, No of Beds = 14, Facilities= WASHING MACHINE, TUMBLE DRYER, BICYCLE STORAGE, INTERNET, PRIVATE ROOMS AVAILABLE
Opening Times: 12:00 till 21:00 April 1 till October 31

### Albergue The Way
Address: A Brea, 36
GPS Coordinates: 42.92031, -8.30465 / 42°55'13"N, 8°18'17"W ·
Telephone: +34 9 8150 2990
Email: info@theway.org.es
Web: www.theway.org.es
Min Cost= €15, No of Beds = 40, Facilities= WASHING MACHINE, TUMBLE DRYER, INTERNET, PRIVATE ROOMS AVAILABLE, SWIMMING POOL.
Opening Times: 13:00 till N/A May 1 till October 31
Booking.com: www.booking.com/hotel/es/pension-the-way.es.html

# Santa Irene

23km to Santiago. 1.4km to A Rua. Altitude 355m. Available Beds=75.
Local Facilities= CAFE/BAR. GPS: 42.91828, -8.33582

## Notes on Santa Irene

About 1km before Santa Irene at the road junction at the top of the
hill (42.91525, -8.322970) there are two nice restaurant/bars where
you can take a break.

## Santa Irene Village Map

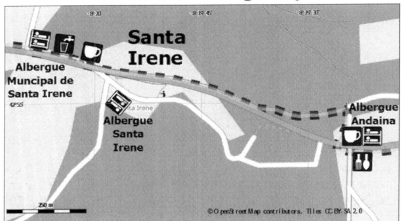

## Pilgrim Accommodation Santa Irene

### Albergue Xunta

Address: Santa Irene, s/n - Arca O Pino
GPS Coordinates: 42.918336, -8.3358 / 42°55'6"N, 8°20'9"W
Telephone: +34 6 6039 6825
Web: camino.xacobeo.es/albergues/albergue-de-santa-irene
Min Cost= €6, No of Beds = 36, Facilities= KITCHEN, WASHING
MACHINE, TUMBLE DRYER, BICYCLE STORAGE
Opening Times: 13:00 till 23:00 January 1 till December 31

### Albergue Rural Astrar

Address: Astrar, 18
GPS Coordinates: 42.91182, -8.3378 / 42°54'43"N, 8°20'16"W
Telephone: +34 9 8151 1463 OR +34 6 0809 2820
Email: albergueruralastrar@gmail.com
Web: www.albergueruralastrar.com

Min Cost= €10, No of Beds = 24, Facilities= KITCHEN, WASHING
MACHINE, TUMBLE DRYER, BICYCLE STORAGE, INTERNET
Opening Times: 11:00 till 23:00 January 1 till December 31

## Albergue Andaina

Address: Empalme de Santa Irene,11
GPS Coordinates: 42.91546, -8.32326 / 42°54'56"N, 8°19'24"W
Telephone: +34 9 8150 2925 OR +34 6 0973 9404
Email: albergue.andaina@gmail.com
Web: www.facebook.com/Andaina-965251216896558
Min Cost= €10, No of Beds = 14, Facilities= WASHING MACHINE,
TUMBLE DRYER, BICYCLE STORAGE, INTERNET
Opening Times: 06:30 till 02:00 January 1 till December 31

## Albergue Santa Irene

Address: Santa Irene, s/n
GPS Coordinates: 42.91703, -8.33228 / 42°55'1"N, 8°19'56"W
Telephone: +34 9 8151 1000
Min Cost= €13, No of Beds = 15, Facilities= WASHING MACHINE,
TUMBLE DRYER, BICYCLE STORAGE, INTERNET
Opening Times: 12:00 till 22:00 April 1 till October 31

# A Rua

22km to Santiago. 2.3km to O Pedrouzo. Altitude 282m. Local
Facilities= CAFE/BAR, RESTAURANT, HOTEL OR GUEST HOUSE TYPE
ACCOMMODATION. GPS: 42.91469, -8.3501

# Pedrouzo (Arca)

20km to Santiago. 2.6km to Amenal. Altitude 262m. Available
Beds=526. Local Facilities= CAFE/BAR, RESTAURANT, ATM, HOTEL
OR GUEST HOUSE TYPE ACCOMMODATION, PHARMACY, MEDICAL
CENTRE, GROCERY STORE. GPS: 42.91205, -8.357725

## Notes on Pedrouzo(Arca)

Pedrouzo is also known as Arca. It is a relatively modern town
though recent excavations have revealed a pilgrim cemetery which is
thought to have been attached to the Hospital de Santa Eulalia de Arca
of which nothing remains. You have to detour off the Camino to enter
the main street in Pedrouzo which has several bars/cafes and
restaurants to service the needs of the pilgrims. As this is the last
major stopping point before Santiago, accommodation is often fully
booked so it is advisable to book in advance as the next major albergue
is another 15 km away.

There are several reasonable restaurants in Pedrouzo but of note is "Taste the Way" which is on the high street and also offers a really good take out service. Although I have not tried it myself I have had several recommendations for the steak at Cafe Bar "O Pedrouzo" on Rúa Concello.

## Pedrouzo(Arca) Town Map

© OpenStreetMap contributors. Tiles CC-BY-SA 2.0

## Pilgrim Accommodation Pedrouzo

### Albergue Xunta de Arca do Pino

Address: O Pedrouzo - Arca, s/n O Pino
GPS Coordinates: 42.907034, -8.35883 / 42°54'25"N, 8°21'32"W
Telephone: +34 6 6039 6826
Web: camino.xacobeo.es/albergues/albergue-de-o-pino
Min Cost= €6, No of Beds = 126, Facilities= INTERNET
Opening Times: 13:00 till 22:00 January 1 till December 31

### Albergue Cruceiro de Pedrouzo
Address: Avenida de la Iglesia 7
GPS Coordinates: 42.90303, -8.36297 / 42°54'11"N, 8°21'47"W
Telephone: +34 9 8151 1371 OR +34 6 2951 8204
Email: reservas@alberguecruceirodepedrouzo.com
Web: www.alberguecruceirodepedrouzo.com
Min Cost= €10, No of Beds = 94, Facilities= KITCHEN, WASHING
MACHINE, TUMBLE DRYER, BICYCLE STORAGE, INTERNET
Opening Times: 12:00 till 23:00 March 1 till November 30

### Porta de Santiago
Address: Avenida de Lugo, 11
GPS Coordinates: 42.90517, -8.36153 / 42°54'19"N, 8°21'42"W
Telephone: +34 9 8151 1103 OR +34 6 0783 5354
Email: portadesantiago@hotmail.com
Web: www.portadesantiago.com
Min Cost= €10, No of Beds = 86, Facilities= KITCHEN, WASHING
MACHINE, TUMBLE DRYER, BICYCLE STORAGE, INTERNET
Opening Times: 12:00 till 23:00 March 1 till November 30

### Albergue Edreira
Address: Rúa da Fonte, 19
GPS Coordinates: 42.90367, -8.36056 / 42°54'13"N, 8°21'38"W
Telephone: +34 9 8151 1365 OR +34 6 6023 4995
Email: info@albergue-edreira.com
Web: www.albergue-edreira.com
Min Cost= €10, No of Beds = 52, Facilities= KITCHEN, WASHING
MACHINE, BICYCLE STORAGE, INTERNET
Opening Times: 12:00 till 23:00 March 1 till October 31

### Albergue O Trisquel
Address: Rúa Picón, 1
GPS Coordinates: 42.90501, -8.3612 / 42°54'18"N, 8°21'40"W
Telephone: +34 6 1664 4740
Email: informatrisquel@gmail.com;
Web: www.facebook.com/o.trisquel.albergue
Min Cost= €10, No of Beds = 68, Facilities= KITCHEN, WASHING
MACHINE, BICYCLE STORAGE, INTERNET
Opening Times: 11:00 till 23:00 March 1 till October 31
Booking.com: www.booking.com/hotel/es/albergue-o-trisquel.html

### Hostel Rem
Address: Avenida da Igrexa 7
GPS Coordinates: 42.90319, -8.36299 / 42°54'11"N, 8°21'47"W
Telephone: +34 9 8151 0407 OR +34 6 1853 3515

Email: reservas@hostelrem.com

Web: hostelrem.com

Min Cost= €10, No of Beds = 40, Facilities= WASHING MACHINE, TUMBLE DRYER, BICYCLE STORAGE, INTERNET

Opening Times: 11:00 till 23:00 April 1 till October 31

## Albergue Otero

Address: Calle de Forcarei, 2

GPS Coordinates: 42.90506, -8.36336 / 42°54'18"N, 8°21'48"W

Telephone: +34 6 7166 3374

Email: info@albergueotero.com

Web: www.albergueotero.com

Min Cost= €10, No of Beds = 36, Facilities= KITCHEN, WASHING MACHINE, TUMBLE DRYER, BICYCLE STORAGE, INTERNET

Opening Times: 11:00 till 23:00 April 1 till November 30

## Albergue Turistico O Burgo

Address: Avenida de Lugo, 47

GPS Coordinates: 42.90905, -8.35874 / 42°54'33"N, 8°21'31"W

Telephone: +34 6 3040 4138 OR +34 9 8151 1406

Email: info@albergueoburgo.es

Web: www.albergueoburgo.es

Min Cost= €10, No of Beds = 24, Facilities= WASHING MACHINE, TUMBLE DRYER, PRIVATE ROOMS AVAILABLE

Opening Times: 12:00 till 23:00 April 1 till November 30

I love the messages of encouragement that you often find scrawled by previous pilgrims. This one translates as "Let nothing worry you".

# Chapter 8 - Pedrouzo to Santiago de Compostela

| | Waypoints Pedrouzo to Santiago de Compostela | | | | | | | | | |
|---|---|---|---|---|---|---|---|---|---|---|
| From | Waypoint | Decimal GPS | DMS GPS | Distance | 3.9 km/hr | 3.9 km/hr + breaks | 4.6 km/hr | 4.6 km/hr + breaks | 5.3 km/hr | 5.3 km/hr + breaks |
| Pedrouzo | Amenal | 42.90519 -8.39158 | 42°54'19"N 8°23'30"W | 2.6km | 0hrs 46mins | 0hrs 56mins | 0hrs 39mins | 0hrs 47mins | 0hrs 34mins | 0hrs 41mins |
| Amenal | San Paio | 42.90870 -8.42616 | 42°54'31"N 8°25'34"W | 4.2km | 1hrs 20mins | 1hrs 36mins | 1hrs 7mins | 1hrs 21mins | 0hrs 58mins | 1hrs 10mins |
| San Paio | Lavacolla | 42.89746 -8.44662 | 42°53'51"N 8°26'48"W | 2.7km | 0hrs 48mins | 0hrs 58mins | 0hrs 41mins | 0hrs 49mins | 0hrs 35mins | 0hrs 42mins |
| Lavacolla | Vilamaior | 42.89215 -8.44982 | 42°53'32"N 8°26'59"W | 0.8km | 0hrs 16mins | 0hrs 20mins | 0hrs 14mins | 0hrs 16mins | 0hrs 12mins | 0hrs 14mins |
| Vilamaior | San Marcos | 42.89130 -8.48937 | 42°53'29"N 8°29'22"W | 3.7km | 1hrs 6mins | 1hrs 20mins | 0hrs 56mins | 1hrs 7mins | 0hrs 49mins | 0hrs 58mins |
| San Marcos | Monte del Gozo | 42.88821 -8.49867 | 42°53'18"N 8°29'55"W | 0.9km | 0hrs 16mins | 0hrs 19mins | 0hrs 13mins | 0hrs 16mins | 0hrs 11mins | 0hrs 14mins |
| Monte del Gozo | Santiago Puerta del Camino | 42.88185 -8.54020 | 42°52'55"N 8°32'25"W | 4.0km | 1hrs 11mins | 1hrs 26mins | 1hrs 0mins | 1hrs 12mins | 0hrs 52mins | 1hrs 3mins |
| Santiago Puerta del Camino | Santiago Cathedral | 42.88069 -8.54537 | 42°52'50"N 8°32'43"W | 0.5km | 0hrs 9mins | 0hrs 11mins | 0hrs 8mins | 0hrs 9mins | 0hrs 7mins | 0hrs 8mins |
| Pedrouzo | Santiago Cathedral | 42.88069 -8.54537 | 42°52'50"N 8°32'43"W | 19.6km | 5hrs 56mins | 7hrs 7mins | 5hrs 2mins | 6hrs 2mins | 4hrs 22mins | 5hrs 14mins |

# Pedrouzo to Santiago de Compostela Elevation Chart

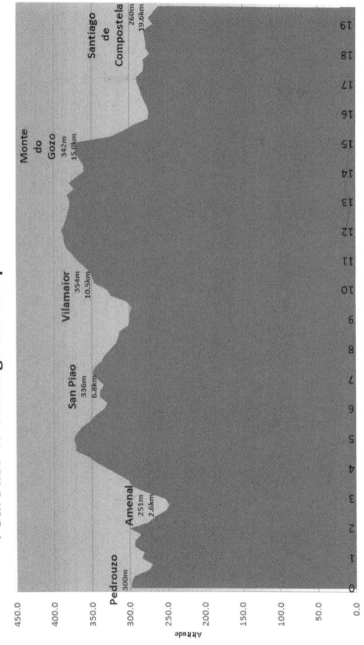

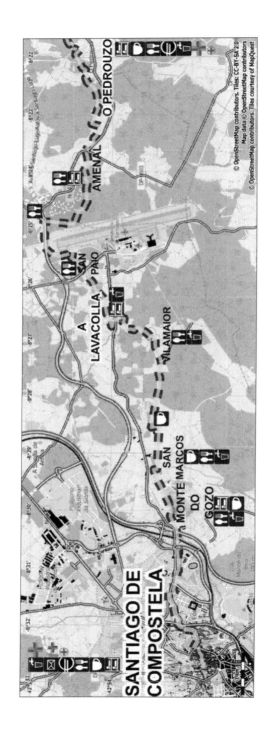

# Notes about Today's Stage

The first part of today's walk is through wooded paths. The trees are particularly tall and there are many Eucalyptus trees among them which makes for very aromatic and pleasant walking. However, it is also particularly dark especially early in the morning so make sure you have a torch with you. The path is littered with mojones (the stone way markers) and is easy to follow even in the dark, with one exception. This exception is at the point where you come out of the woods where the nearest mojón is about 200m down on the left and is not easily visible.

There is just one other albergue (in Lavacolla) on this leg apart from the huge albergue at Monte do Gozo but there are a few cafe/bars along the way where you can grab some breakfast or just take a break. The atmosphere is often buzzing with groups singing along the final leg of their pilgrimage. By this stage most of the other Caminos have joined together so it is a busy stage and better for celebratory walking rather than reflective walking you may have enjoyed earlier in the week. On the way up to Monte do Gozo you will pass the local TV stations. On arriving at Monte de Gozo you will see a large monument which commemorates the visit of Pope John Paul 2 in 1989 and St Francis of Assisi's pilgrimage in 1214. The Monte do Gozo grounds are large and not of great architectural merit with the exception of the viewing point (mirador). This mirador consists of two very large statues of medieval pilgrims catching their first excited view of the cathedral at Santiago. It is a bit of a detour to visit the viewing point so most pilgrims skip this and head straight for Santiago. You are now on the outskirts of the city and like most city walking, walking on concrete is tiring on the feet. Although Santiago appears close, it will take you another 80 minutes before you arrive at your final destination, the cathedral.

# Amenal

17km to Santiago. 4.2km to San Paio. Altitude 251m. Local Facilities=RESTAURANT, HOTEL OR GUEST HOUSE TYPE ACCOMMODATION. GPS: <u>42.905304, -8.391573</u>

## Notes on Amenal

The café/bar of the small hotel at Amenal opens at 7am during the winter and 6am during the summer months and if you are leaving Pedrouzo before 6am to catch the pilgrim's mass this may be your first opportunity for breakfast. The Camino passes by the side of the hotel and after about 2km you will come across the perimeter of the airport. You will then walk around the end of the airport (including underneath the end of the runway) around to the other side.

# San Paio

13km to Santiago. 2.7km to Lavacolla. Altitude 334m. Local Facilities= RESTAURANT. GPS: <u>42.908913, -8.426128</u>

## Notes on San Paio

If you miss the right turn to San Paio you can end up at the airport terminal. If you do end up at the airport terminal you just follow the signposts for Santiago and you eventually end up back on the Camino. By the time, you have reached San Paio most, but not all, of the Caminos have come together so numbers will have significantly increased. The one cafe/bar/hotel in San Paio (called A Casa de Porta de Santiago) if its open, will insist you buy something if you want to use the toilets as there is often a big demand for toilets at this stop. The church next door dates from 1840 and is built on the site of a 12th century monastery. Often there are stalls setup outside selling all kinds of pilgrim mementoes and jewellery. The village and the church is dedicated to San Paio (also known as San Payo or San Pelayo) who was a young boy from Tui/Tuy in Galicia who was martyred in 925 by being pulled apart by iron tongs for refusing to renounce his Christian faith.

# Lavacolla

10km to Santiago. 0.8km to Vilamaior. Altitude 298m. Available Beds=34. Local Facilities=HOTEL OR GUEST HOUSE TYPE ACCOMMODATION. GPS: <u>42.899786, -8.44662</u>

## Pilgrim Accommodation Lavacolla

### Albergue Lavacolla

Address: Lavacolla 35

GPS Coordinates: <u>42.89948, -8.44387</u> / 42°53'58"N, 8°26'38"W
Telephone: <u>+34 9 8189 7274</u> OR <u>+34 6 5363 0300</u>
Email: <u>reservas@alberguelavacolla.com</u>
Web: <u>www.alberguelavacolla.com</u>
Min Cost= €12, No of Beds = 34, Facilities= KITCHEN, BICYCLE STORAGE, INTERNET
Opening Times: 13:30 till 21:00 April 1 till November 30

## Notes on Lavacolla

Lavacolla is described in the Codex Calixtinus as the place where pilgrims would take off all their clothes and wash themselves in the river. This was done out of respect for and in preparation for meeting Saint James. Even after a few days it is possible to appreciate that maintaining personal hygiene standards whilst living out of a back pack and walking 23km per day is challenging. However, I am not sure this is a tradition I would like to see come back into fashion as the river in question is a very small stream these days, completely unsuitable for bathing.

# Vilamaior

9km to Santiago. 3.7km to San Marcos. Altitude 351m. Local Facilities=RESTAURANT. GPS: <u>42.892151, -8.449825</u>

## Notes on Vilamaior

Some pilgrims choose to run up the last 4 or 5 km to the statue at Monte de Gozo from this point; I do not.

# San Marcos

6km to Santiago. 0.9km to Monte do Gozo. Altitude 361m. Local Facilities= CAFE/BAR, RESTAURANT, HOTEL OR GUEST HOUSE TYPE ACCOMMODATION. GPS: <u>42.891202, -8.489444</u>

## Notes on San Marcos

The camping site cafe/bar on the corner at the very start of San Marcos is the last rest stop before Santiago itself.

# Monte do Gozo

5km to Santiago. 4.6km to Santiago de Compostela. Altitude 339m. Available Beds=440. Local Facilities= CAFE/BAR, RESTAURANT. GPS: <u>42.88741, -8.49817</u>

## Notes on Monte do Gozo

Monte de Gozo means mount of joy and refers to the joy that most pilgrims feel at reaching the top of this last hill before Santiago. The atmosphere is really buzzing by this point. Tradition holds that even those who have made the pilgrimage on horseback dismount and walk the last 4 or 5 km in by foot. It is not a tradition that has yet been adopted by the bicigrinos but I think it would make a nice tradition if all pilgrims could walk in together as one.

If you want to enjoy the traditional view that medieval pilgrims enjoyed of Santiago, it is about a 10-minute detour to the mirador with the two huge pilgrim statues. As the route from the mirador back on to the Camino is not marked I would suggest after visiting the mirador to head back to the main (JP II/Saint Francis) monument and re-join the Camino there.

From here on in its downhill pretty much all the way and after many days of uphill and downhill that is a joy in itself. From here also you are on the outskirts of the city and as any seasoned walker will tell you city walking is the most draining as it is literally hard on your feet. As you get closer there are progressively more bars and cafes where you can give your poor feet 5 minutes rest and enjoy a soft drink before the final push into the centre of Praça do Obradoiro where your pilgrimage officially ends.

Please note that for security reasons you will not be allowed into the cathedral with a full backpack although you may be allowed in with a small daypack which will be searched. However, if you have a backpack there is no problem as next to the entrance to the cathedral on the corner is a facility where for a small fee they will store your backpack for several hours giving you time to visit the cathedral, go to the Pilgrim's Office to get your Compostela and have some lunch before you head off to find your accommodation.

# Monte do Gozo Village Map

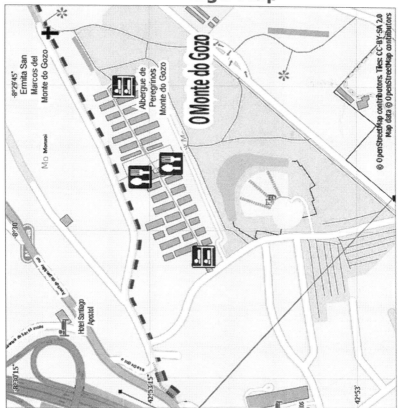

## Pilgrim Accommodation Monte do Gozo

### Albergue Xunta del Monte do Gozo

Address: Carretera del Aeropuerto, 2km
GPS Coordinates: <u>42.88722, -8.499886</u> / 42°53'14"N, 8°29'60"W
Telephone: <u>+34 6 6039 6827</u>
Web: <u>camino.xacobeo.es/albergues/albergue-de-monte-do-gozo</u>
Min Cost= €6, No of Beds = 400, Facilities= BICYCLE STORAGE
Opening Times: 13:00 till 22:00 January 1 till December 31

### John Paul II (Polish Albergue)

Address: Rúa das Estrelas, 80
GPS Coordinates: <u>42.88694, -8.49382</u> / 42°53'13"N, 8°29'38"W
Telephone: <u>+34 9 8159 7222</u>
Email: <u>ceperegrinacion@alfaexpress.net</u>

124
Web: www.albergue.pl
Min Cost= €Don, No of Beds = 40, Facilities= KITCHEN, BICYCLE
STORAGE, COMMUNAL MEAL
Opening Times: 13:00 till 22:00 January 1 till December 31

# Chapter 9 - Santiago de Compostela

0km to Santiago. Altitude 261m. Available Beds=843. Local Facilities= CAFE/BAR, RESTAURANT, ATM, HOTEL OR GUEST HOUSE TYPE ACCOMMODATION, PHARMACY, MEDICAL CENTRE, GROCERY STORE. GPS: <u>42.88059, -8.545186</u>

# Large Map of Santiago

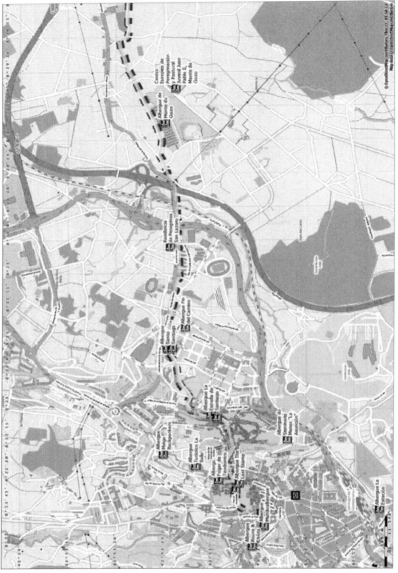

# Map of Central Santiago

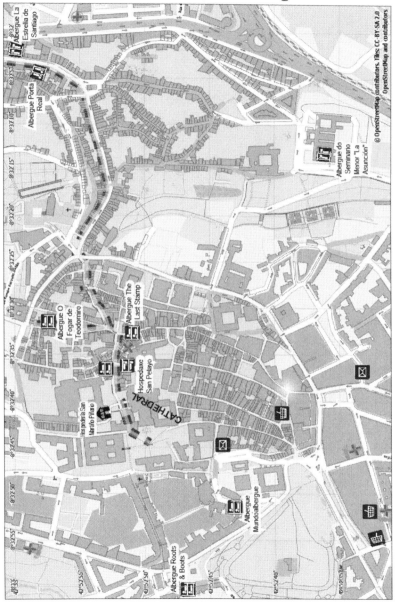

Albergue La Estrella de Santiago

Albergue Porta Real

Albergue do Seminario Menor "La Asunción"

Albergue O Fogar de Teodomiro

Albergue The Last Stamp

Hospedaxe San Pelayo

Hospedería San Martín Pinario

CATHEDRAL

Albergue Mundoalbergue

Albergue Roots & Boots

# Pilgrim Accommodation Santiago de Compostela

## Albergue Jaime García Rodríguez

Address: Rúa de Moscova
GPS Coordinates: 42.88528, -8.52333 / 42°53'7"N, 8°31'24"W
Telephone: +34 9 8158 7324
Email: albergue@fundacionperegrinacionasantiago.com
Min Cost= €8, No of Beds = 150, Facilities= KITCHEN, WASHING
MACHINE, TUMBLE DRYER, BICYCLE STORAGE, INTERNET
Opening Times: 11:30 till 00:00 May 1 till September 30

## Albergue Xunta San Lazaro

Address: Rúa San Lázaro
GPS Coordinates: 42.887386, -8.51322 / 42°53'15"N, 8°30'48"W
Telephone: +34 9 8157 1488 OR +34 6 1826 6894
Web: camino.xacobeo.es/albergues/albergue-residencia-de-peregrinos-de-san-lazaro
Min Cost= €10, No of Beds = 80, Facilities= KITCHEN, WASHING
MACHINE, TUMBLE DRYER, BICYCLE STORAGE
Opening Times: 09:00 till 22:00 January 1 till December 31

## Albergue Acuario

Address: Estocolmo 2
GPS Coordinates: 42.88669, -8.52533 / 42°53'12"N, 8°31'31"W
Telephone: +34 9 8157 5438
Email: reservas@acuariosantiago.com
Web: www.acuariosantiago.com
Min Cost= €10, No of Beds = 70, Facilities= KITCHEN, WASHING
MACHINE, TUMBLE DRYER, BICYCLE STORAGE, INTERNET
Opening Times: 09:00 till 00:00 February 15 till December 15
Booking.com: www.booking.com/hotel/es/albergue-acuario.html

## Albergue Santo Santiago

Address: Rúa do Valiño, 3
GPS Coordinates: 42.88711, -8.52592 / 42°53'14"N, 8°31'33"W
Telephone: +34 6 5740 2403
Email: elsantosantiago@gmail.com
Web: www.elsantosantiago.com
Min Cost= €10, No of Beds = 40, Facilities= WASHING MACHINE,
TUMBLE DRYER, BICYCLE STORAGE, INTERNET
Opening Times: 09:00 till N/A January 1 till December 31

## Albergue La Credencial

Address: Fonte dos Concheiros, 13 Bajo

GPS Coordinates: 42.88525, -8.53222 / 42°53'7"N, 8°31'56"W
Telephone: +34 9 8106 8083 OR +34 6 3996 6704
Email: reservaslacredencial@gmail.com
Web: www.lacredencial.es
Min Cost= €10, No of Beds = 36, Facilities= KITCHEN, WASHING
MACHINE, TUMBLE DRYER, BICYCLE STORAGE, INTERNET
Opening Times: 11:00 till 22:00 March 1 till November 30
Booking.com: www.booking.com/hotel/es/albergue-turistico-la-
credencial.es.html

### Albergue La Estrella de Santiago

Address: Rúa Concheiros, 36-38
GPS Coordinates: 42.88321, -8.53415 / 42°52'60"N, 8°32'3"W
Telephone: +34 6 1788 2529 OR +34 8 8197 3926
Email: laestrelladesantiago@hotmail.com
Web: www.laestrelladesantiago.es
Min Cost= €10, No of Beds = 24, Facilities= KITCHEN, WASHING
MACHINE
Opening Times: 09:00 till 22:00 January 1 till December 31

### Albergue Porta Real

Address: Rúa dos Concheiros, 10
GPS Coordinates: 42.88222, -8.53462 / 42°52'56"N, 8°32'5"W
Telephone: +34 6 3361 0114
Email: reservas@albergueportareal.es
Web: albergueportareal.es
Min Cost= €10, No of Beds = 20, Facilities= WASHING MACHINE,
TUMBLE DRYER, BICYCLE STORAGE
Opening Times: N/A till N/A January 1 till December 31

### Albergue Seminario Menor de Belvis

Address: Avenida Quiroga Palacios
GPS Coordinates: 42.877206, -8.537332 / 42°52'38"N, 8°32'14"W
Telephone: +34 8 8103 1768 OR +34 9 8156 8521
Email: santiago@alberguesdelcamino.com
Web: www.alberguesdelcamino.com
Min Cost= €12, No of Beds = 177, Facilities= KITCHEN, WASHING
MACHINE, TUMBLE DRYER, BICYCLE STORAGE, INTERNET, PRIVATE
ROOMS AVAILABLE
Opening Times: 13:30 till 00:00 March 1 till October 31
Booking.com: www.booking.com/hotel/es/albergue-seminario-
menor.html

### Albergue Meiga Backpackers

Address: Rúa Baquiños, 67

GPS Coordinates: 42.88742, -8.53885 / 42°53'15"N, 8°32'20"W
Telephone: +34 9 8157 0846
Email: info_meiga@yahoo.es
Web: www.meiga-backpackers.es
Min Cost= €13, No of Beds = 18, Facilities= WASHING MACHINE,
TUMBLE DRYER, BICYCLE STORAGE, INTERNET
Opening Times: 10:00 till 22:00 January 7 till December 23

## Albergue Blanco

Address: Rúa das Galeras, 30
GPS Coordinates: 42.8819, -8.54888 / 42°52'55"N, 8°32'56"W
Telephone: +34 8 8197 6850 OR +34 6 9959 1238
Email: prblanco@prblanco.com
Web: www.prblanco.com
Min Cost= €12, No of Beds = 20, Facilities= KITCHEN, WASHING
MACHINE, TUMBLE DRYER, BICYCLE STORAGE, INTERNET, PRIVATE
ROOMS AVAILABLE
Opening Times: 12:00 till N/A January 1 till December 31
Booking.com: www.booking.com/hotel/es/blanco-albergue.html

## Albergue Basquinos 45

Address: Rúa dos Basquiños, 45
GPS Coordinates: 42.88719, -8.53922 / 42°53'14"N, 8°32'21"W
Telephone: +34 6 6189 4536
Email: albergueb45@gmail.com
Min Cost= €12, No of Beds = 10, Facilities= WASHING MACHINE,
TUMBLE DRYER, BICYCLE STORAGE, INTERNET
Opening Times: 12:00 till N/A January 1 till December 31
Booking.com: www.booking.com/hotel/es/albergue-basquinos-
45.en-gb.html

## Albergue La Estacion

Address: Rúa Xoana Nogueira, 14
GPS Coordinates: 42.86856, -8.5458 / 42°52'7"N, 8°32'45"W
Telephone: +34 9 8159 4624 OR +34 6 3922 8617
Email: info@alberguelaestacion.com
Web: www.alberguelaestacion.com
Min Cost= €14, No of Beds = 24, Facilities= KITCHEN, WASHING
MACHINE, TUMBLE DRYER, BICYCLE STORAGE, INTERNET, PRIVATE
ROOMS AVAILABLE
Opening Times: 13:00 till 00:00 Holy Week till September 30

## Albergue Monterrey

Address: Rúa das Fontiñas, 65, Bajo
GPS Coordinates: 42.88629, -8.52839 / 42°53'11"N, 8°31'42"W

Telephone: +34 8 8112 5093 OR +34 6 5548 4299
Email: alberguemonterrey@gmail.com
Web: alberguemonterrey.es
Min Cost= €14, No of Beds = 36, Facilities= KITCHEN, WASHING
MACHINE, TUMBLE DRYER, BICYCLE STORAGE, INTERNET
Opening Times: 12:00 till 22:00 January 1 till December 31
Booking.com: www.booking.com/hotel/es/albergue-
monterrey.es.html

## Albergue The last Stamp

Address: Rúa Preguntorio, 10
GPS Coordinates: 42.88089, -8.54246 / 42°52'51"N, 8°32'33"W
Telephone: +34 9 8156 3525
Email: reservas@thelaststamp.es
Web: www.thelaststamp.es
Min Cost= €15, No of Beds = 62, Facilities= KITCHEN, WASHING
MACHINE, TUMBLE DRYER, BICYCLE STORAGE, INTERNET
Opening Times: 14:00 till N/A January 16 till December 14
Booking.com: www.booking.com/hotel/es/the-last-stamp.html

## Albergue Compostela

Address: San Pedro de Mezonzo, 28 Bajo
GPS Coordinates: 42.87219, -8.54795 / 42°52'20"N, 8°32'53"W
Telephone: +34 8 8101 7840
Email: contacto@alberguecompostela.es
Web: www.alberguecompostela.es
Min Cost= €15, No of Beds = 40, Facilities= KITCHEN, WASHING
MACHINE, TUMBLE DRYER, BICYCLE STORAGE, INTERNET
Opening Times: 12:00 till 22:00 January 1 till December 31
Booking.com: www.booking.com/hotel/es/albergue-
compostela.es.html

## Albergue Roots & Boots

Address: Rúa Campo de Cruceiro do Galo, 7
GPS Coordinates: 42.879, -8.54979 / 42°52'44"N, 8°32'59"W
Telephone: +34 6 9963 1594
Email: info@rootsandboots.es
Web: www.rootsandboots.es
Min Cost= €15, No of Beds = 48, Facilities= WASHING MACHINE,
TUMBLE DRYER, INTERNET
Opening Times: 09:00 till N/A January 1 till December 31
Booking.com: www.booking.com/hotel/es/roots.html

## Albergue O Fogar de Teodormiro

Address: Plaza de Algalia de Arriba, 3

GPS Coordinates: 42.88266, -8.542153 / 42°52'58"N, 8°32'32"W
Telephone: +34 9 8158 2920 OR +34 6 9963 1592
Email: fogarteodomiro@aldahostels.es
Web: www.fogarteodomiro.com
Min Cost= €16.49, No of Beds = 20, Facilities= KITCHEN, WASHING
MACHINE, TUMBLE DRYER, BICYCLE STORAGE, INTERNET
Opening Times: 10:00 till 23:00 January 1 till December 31
Booking.com: www.booking.com/hotel/es/o-fogar-de-
teodomiro.html

## Albergue La Salle

Address: Tras Santa Clara
GPS Coordinates: 42.88482, -8.54043 / 42°53'5"N, 8°32'26"W
Telephone: +34 6 8215 8011 OR +34 6 8215 8011
Email: info@alberguelasalle.com
Web: www.alberguelasalle.com
Min Cost= €17, No of Beds = 20, Facilities= KITCHEN, WASHING
MACHINE, TUMBLE DRYER, BICYCLE STORAGE, INTERNET
Opening Times: N/A till N/A January 1 till December 31

## Albergue Mundoalbergue

Address: Calle San Clemente, 26
GPS Coordinates: 42.87863, -8.54754 / 42°52'43"N, 8°32'51"W
Telephone: +34 9 8158 8625 OR +34 6 9644 8737
Web: www.mundoalbergue.es
Min Cost= €18, No of Beds = 34, Facilities= KITCHEN, WASHING
MACHINE, TUMBLE DRYER, BICYCLE STORAGE, INTERNET
Opening Times: 12:00 till N/A January 1 till December 31

## Albergue Azabache

Address: Rúa Acibechería 15
GPS Coordinates: 42.88122, -8.54354 / 42°52'52"N, 8°32'37"W
Telephone: +34 9 8107 1254
Email: azabachehostel@yahoo.es
Web: www.azabache-santiago.com
Min Cost= €18, No of Beds = 20, Facilities= KITCHEN, WASHING
MACHINE, TUMBLE DRYER, BICYCLE STORAGE
Opening Times: 12:00 till 22:00 January 1 till December 31

# What to see and do when in Santiago?

## The Pilgrim's Mass

The pilgrim's mass in Santiago is at 12:00 each day and is a fantastic experience. Whilst it might not to be to everyone's taste or inclination, it is part of the pilgrimage experience and it is worth experiencing at least once. The mass normally lasts about 50 minutes.

## Confession and Plenary Indulgences

Please bear with me on this as this is a difficult topic to explain to Catholics let alone other Christians or people of other faiths. So, if you are not religiously inclined you may want to skip this section or read it out of curiosity alone. Either way I will try and explain this part of the pilgrimage experience as best I can.

Put simply, the Church teaches that sins (wrong doings against other people) keep people away from God. The Church also teaches that if you simply but honestly say sorry to God (via the priest in Confession) your sins will be forgiven. The church teaches that if your sins are forgiven you will go to heaven. However, you will still have to atone for your sins by spending time after your death in a waiting room called Purgatory before you finally get into heaven. The Church also teaches that you can reduce or eliminate this waiting time by means of what is called a papal indulgence which is given for undertaking a task to atone for your sins while still on earth. There are two types of papal indulgence a partial indulgence which reduces the waiting time or a plenary (full) which completely eliminates this waiting time. Initially plenary indulgences were only given to those who died on pilgrimage.

What's all this got to do with the Camino? Well in 1122, Pope Calixtus II (the Pope who supposedly commissioned the Codex Calixtinus) granted a full (plenary) indulgence for anyone who visited the shrine of Saint James in Santiago de Compostela in the years when the saint's day (July 25th) fell on a Sunday, made a confession whilst there, attended Mass, gave a donation to the upkeep of the shrine and performed good works. This indulgence is still available in a slightly modernised form for anyone who simply visits (there is no need to do a Camino) the Cathedral of Santiago and the tomb of Saint James in a Jacobean Holy Year. These Jacobean Holy Years occur when the feast of Saint James falls on a Sunday – for example 2004, 2010, 2021 and 2027. To complete the qualification for a modern plenary indulgence you must within 15 days either before or after your visit to the Cathedral make a true confession, receive Holy Communion (but not necessarily go to Mass), pray at least the Our Father and the Apostles Creed and pray for the intentions of the Pope. Any visits during the special Holy Year of Mercy (2016) also qualified for the plenary indulgence. But if you can't make it to Santiago during a Holy Year, you can still obtain the indulgence by visiting on one of Saint James's feast days (23rd May, 25th July, or 30th December).

Even if you are of no faith, virtually all priests, whilst not officially administering confession will minister to you and listen in confidence to anything that burdens you.

Confession is available throughout the day at the many confessionals around the cathedral. If there are no priests in the confessionals, or you are seeking confession in your own language, please ask in the sacristy.

## The Botafumeiro

The Botafumeiro is one of two giant (1.5 metres tall) incense burners (thuribles) used at the end of the pilgrims' mass to incense the Cathedral. Botafumeiro is a Galician word that literally means "ejector of smoke".

The current Botafumeiro dates from 1851 and was built to replace the even more ornate 15th century Botafumeiro stolen by Napoleon's troops in 1809. It weighs 53kg and can take up to 40kg of charcoal and incense. It travels to a height of 21 metres and up to speeds of 80 km/hr. It is swung on a rope and pulley system by seven men. There are no known fatalities from the Botafumeiro becoming detached from the ropes but there have been several non-fatal accidents in the past where the Botafumeiro did become fully or partially detached. The last of these accidents was in 1937.

The other large thurible, called the La Alcachofa (The Artichoke), is a replica of the one stolen by Napoleon and dates from 1971.

The Botafumeiro is swung every Friday (except Good Friday) at the 7:30pm mass and on most major holy days. It is not swung every day at the midday mass but since it is such a spectacular sight and one of the highlights of any visit to Santiago, increasingly many groups of pilgrims collect the €450 donation required to secure the swinging of the Botafumeiro or the Alcachofa at the end of the midday mass. If you are part of a group and wish to organise the swinging, the Cathedral ask for one week's notice. The contact for organising the swinging of the Botafumeiro is: botafumeiro@catedraldesantiago.es .

## The Pilgrims' Office

The pilgrims' office is where you get your final stamp and your Compostela certificate of completion which is free. Most pilgrims also pay €3 for a certificate of distance and €2 for a round box to take your certificate home rolled up safely.

The pilgrims' office moved at the end of 2015 to larger offices to accommodate the ever-increasing number of pilgrims.

To enter the pilgrims' office, you will need to show your pilgrim's passport. Be prepared to wait as the queue (line) for getting your Compostela can often exceed two hours. The best time to avoid long queues is early morning. In fact, if you are among the first 10 pilgrims to collect your Compostela that day you will be given a certificate for a free lunch at the Parador!

The pilgrims' office is open 08:00 till 21:00 from April till October and from 10:00 till 19:00 for the rest of the year.

The new pilgrims' office includes a post office, a RENFE (the Spanish national railway company) office and an ALSA (the largest of the bus companies) office.

## Location of Pilgrims' Office

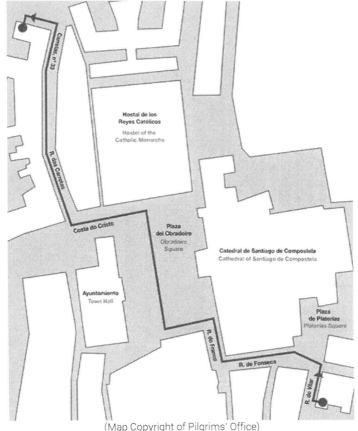

(Map Copyright of Pilgrims' Office)

Address: Rúa Carretas, 33
GPS Coordinates: 42.88233, -8.54714/ 42°52'56"N,8°32'50"W
Telephone: +34 9 8156 8846
Email: info@peregrinossantiago.es
Web: www.peregrinossantiago.es/eng/pilgrims-office/welcome/
Summer Opening Times: 08:00 till 21:00 April 1st till October 30th
Winter Opening Times: 10:00 till 19:00 November 1st till March 30th

## The Cathedral Museum

The entrance to the Cathedral museum is located on the Praça do Obradoiro to the right as you look at the Cathedral. It takes you through the history of the building of the Cathedral which is rich and varied as well as through some of the art and treasures of the Cathedral. The tour takes at least two hours and an audio guide is highly recommended.

Address: Praza do Obradoiro, s/n
GPS Coordinates: 42.880084, -8.545210
Telephone: +34 9 8155 2985
Web: www.catedraldesantiago.es/en/node/469
Summer (April till October) Monday to Sunday Opening Times: 09:00 till 20:00
Winter (November till March) Monday to Sunday Opening Times: 10:00 till 20:00
Cost: €6.00 or €4.00 for concessions.

## The Pilgrimage Museum

The pilgrimage museum is housed in the beautiful former Banco de Espana building (designed in 1938 but only completed in 1948) located near the south-east corner of the Cathedral buildings. The museum covers 3 floors on the generic theme of pilgrimage but mainly focused on the history of the Camino. On the top floor you get a good view of the top of the Cathedral which is quite impressive. A tour of the museum should take about an hour. This is my personal favourite amongst the museums in Santiago.

Address: Praza das Praterías, 2
GPS Coordinates: 42.879947, -8.544153
Telephone: +34 9 8156 6110
Email: difusion.mdperegrinacions@xunta.es
Web: museoperegrinacions.xunta.gal/
Monday to Friday Opening Times: 09:30 till 20:30
Saturday Opening Times: 11:00 till 19:00
Sunday and Public Holidays Opening Times: 10:15 till 14:45

Cost: €2.40 or €1.20 with your Compostela. Also, free Saturday afternoon from 14:30 and all day Sunday and for over 65s.

## The Galician Museum of Modern Art

This modern buildings dates from 1993. Personally, I like the granite facade and its clean lines but it is not to everyone's taste. The museum's permanent collection mainly focuses on Galician, Spanish, Portuguese and Latin American artists.

Address: Rúa Valle Inclán, 2
GPS Coordinates: 42.882514, -8.539448
Telephone: +34 9 8154 6619
Email: cgac.prensa@xunta.gal
Web: cgac.xunta.gal/
Tuesday to Sunday Opening Times: 11:00 till 20:00
Closed Mondays
Cost: Free.

## "Free" Walking Tours of Santiago

The walking tours leave at 10:00 and 11:00 from the Praça do Obradoiro (the biggest of the four squares around the Cathedral and the one with the Parador in it). There will probably be several tour guides each holding an umbrella and you just have to check that the tour is in English (which most are). The tours are "free" in the sense there is no obligation to pay the guide anything, but the expectation is that you give the tour guide a generous tip at the end of the tour depending on how much you thought the tour was worth. The tours last about two hours and I think provide a good balance between the background and history of Santiago. The tour starts slowly but there is quite a bit of walking involved. Overall highly recommended if you have the time.

## The restaurants

There are good restaurants all over Santiago, but the main restaurant area is Rúa da Raiña and Rúa do Franco which both lead directly south from the Cathedral both parallel to Rúa do Vilar (where the pilgrims' office used to be). There is so much good seafood, meat and cheese in Santiago it is hard to highlight just one or two dishes. But for me my favourite is the gambas al ajillo (prawns fried in garlic infused olive oil) which I have tried across much of Spain but always seems to taste best in Santiago.

My favourite restaurant, however, is to be found outside of the main restaurant area, south west of Praça do Obradoiro and is called Restaurante San Clemente. Beware the tapas are the most generous in Santiago and can easily fill you up before you can order a proper meal.

Address: Rúa de San Clemente, 6
GPS Coordinates: 42.87915, -8.54702
Telephone: +34 9 8156 5426
Web: www.restaurantesanclemente.com

## The bars

There are great bars all over Santiago. But a couple stand out for me:

**Cafe Bar Derby** has a great Art Noveau interior and it is where I first discovered the sinful pleasure of churros con chocolate on my first visit to Santiago in 1993.
Address: Rúa das Orfas, 29
GPS Coordinates: 42.877010, -8.544157
Telephone: +34 9 8158 6417

**Cafe Casino**. Dating from 1873, this is a fabulous example of an early Art Noveau cafe; its wood panelling wreaks of former glory. It has a reputation for some of the best coffee in Santiago but it also has a very extensive gin menu (with some great guest gins which don't make it on to the main menu and you may need to ask after). It is expensive and the food and particularly the service are variable but it is still one of my favourite places to visit in Santiago.
Address: Rúa do Vilar, 35
GPS Coordinates: 42.878640, -8.544542
Telephone: +34 9 8157 7503

**Cafeteria Paradiso**. This hidden gem is only a few doors down from the Cafe Casino but it is family run and has better food, better service and better prices than the Cafe Casino. While the decor may not compete with the Cafe Casino for grandeur, this bar definitely oozes old world charm.
Address: Rúa do Vilar, 29
GPS Coordinates: 42.87879, -8.54445
Telephone: +34 9 8158 3394

## Santiago de Compostela tourist information centre

The tourist information centre is situated on Rúa Vilar which is the road that leads south from the cathedral. It is about 250 metres south of the fountain on the south side of the cathedral in the arches on the right-hand side as you walk down.

The staff are exceptionally helpful and can help you find accommodation, bus and train timetables, how to get to the airport, day trips and details of the many places to see and visit while in Santiago. I would put this third of places to check out when you arrive, with the cathedral being number one and the pilgrims' office number two.

Address: Rúa do Vilar, 63
GPS Coordinates: 42.877956, -8.545038
Telephone: +34 9 8155 5129
Email: info@santiagoturismo.com
Web: www.santiagoturismo.com/
Monday to Sunday Opening Times: 09:00 till 21:00 (May to October)
Monday to Friday Opening Times: 09:00 till 19:00 (November to April)
Saturday, Sunday, Holy Days Opening Times: 09:00 till 14:00 and 16:00 till 19:00 (November to April)
Monday to Sunday Opening Times: 09:00 till 19:00 (Easter)

## Finistera

Finistera translates from Latin meaning the end of the earth and for people of Roman and pre-Roman times, the wild rugged coast at one of the most western points of the known world at the time must have literally felt it was the end of the earth. Even today that feeling of being right at the end of the earth resonates. Many pilgrims feel they have not completed their Camino until they have walked the extra three or four days to Finistera. However, many pilgrims will not enjoy the luxury of an extra four days to extend their Camino to Finistera but for these pilgrims and the many visitors to Santiago there are numerous day trips available to Finistera. These day trips are normally guided coach trips which leave Santiago about 9am and return about 6 or 7pm so they are a long day. These guided tours cost in the range of 35 to 50 euros and usually include a visit to Muxía (with its Sanctuary of the Virgen de la Barca where the final scenes of the film The Way were filmed) and Ézaro (where the waterfall falls directly into the ocean). This is an expensive day trip, but the scenery is spectacular and makes it worthwhile.

# The remains of Saint James in the Crypt of the Cathedral

Everybody goes up stairs above the altar to hug the statue of St James but not quite as many make the trip downstairs below the altar to visit the remains of Saint James. I think this is a bit of a shame as the few moments you get before the remains of Saint James can be among the most calming and prayerful of your whole Camino. Having said that, I don't want to diminish those who have no religious feelings as the Camino is a great experience for all and even if you do not want to participate in any of the religious aspects I still believe the Camino is a fabulous experience on and of its own.

# Chapter 10 - Background

## *Statistics*

### Pilgrim Numbers starting in Sarria by Month

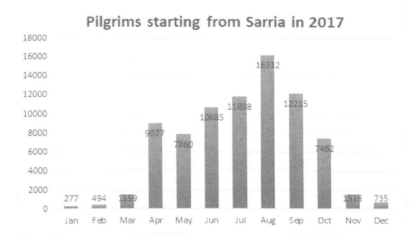

### Pilgrim Numbers by Year

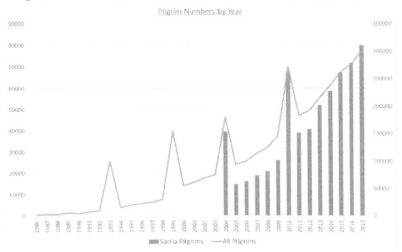

# *History*

## A brief history of the Remains of Saint James

There are two apostles called James both saints. The Saint James in Santiago is also known as James the Greater, not because he is deemed to be a better saint than James the Less but because he was simply taller that James the Less. James was one of the fishermen called by Jesus along with his brother John. James and John were sons of Zebedee and Salome. He and John were the first apostles to be called. James was one of the chosen apostles to witness the Transfiguration of Jesus. Tradition holds that after the Resurrection that James went to the Roman province of Hispania (modern day Spain and Portugal) to spread the Gospel. It is held that St James first preached in Galicia in the port of Iria Flavia (modern day Padrón, now more famous for its delicious green peppers). He returned to the Holy Land where he was beheaded by Herod Agrippa in AD 44 and was the first of the apostles to be martyred as recorded in the Acts of the Apostles 12:2. Tradition holds that his body was taken from Jerusalem by his followers, Theodore and Athanasius back to the land where he had spent most of his ministry and which he had grown to love. It is believed that his body was bought back ashore at Iria Flavia. The story goes that Theodore and Athanasius approached the local King for permission to bury St James's body somewhere appropriate. However, the King's wife, Queen Lupa who was not keen on her husband's conversion to Christianity sent Theodore and Athanasius to collect two oxen to pull the wagon with St James's body to a suitable resting place in the countryside (Santiago). The oxen were in fact wild bulls which Queen Lupa had hoped would do away with Theodore and Athanasius and any devotion to the remains of St James. However, the wild bulls were miraculously tamed and upon seeing this, the legend holds that Queen Lupa was also converted to Christianity and dedicated the rest of her life to doing good deeds.

## A brief history of the Camino

There are some written references about the remains of St James being buried in Galicia during the Dark Ages. This written evidence of the belief that St James was buried in Galicia dates from at least two hundred years prior to the discovery of the remains in Santiago.

The remains of St James remained undiscovered for over seven centuries until 813 when according to legend a hermit named Pelayo had a vision repeated over several evenings. According to the legend Pelayo lived in a place called Solovio, in the forest of Libredón in what is believed to be the current day site of the church of San Félix de Solovio. This church is to be found in Praza de San Fiz de Solvio which is just a few hundred metres south east of the Cathedral in modern day Santiago de Compostela. The dazzling vision revealed to Pelayo was of a mysterious blaze above a mound in the forest which gave the impression of a field of stars (Compostela literally translates to field of stars). This vision occurred in what is now the site of the Cathedral of Santiago (Santiago is Galician for Saint James). Hence Santiago received the name Santiago de Compostela (Saint James of the Field of Stars). Pelayo went to the local bishop Teodormiro and told of his vision. Teodormiro prayed and fasted for guidance and then went to Santiago and discovered a sepulchre containing 3 bodies. After various miracles Teodormiro pronounced this to be the remains of Saint James and his two faithful followers Theodore and Athanasius. He relayed his findings to King Alfonso II of Asturias (791-842) who ordered the building of the first church on the site in 834. There are some problems with this version of events not least of which was that Teodormiro did not become bishop till 819. It is thought the 813 date may be an attempt to link the start of the Camino to the Emperor Charlemagne (800-814). In the Charlemagne version of the discovery of the tomb of Saint James, Saint James appeared in a dream to Charlemagne and asked Charlemagne to liberate the lands held and open up the way to his tomb.

Gaining in popularity is a tradition that the Camino itself predates the Way of Saint James and that in pre-Christian times that the Camino was a spiritual trail which follows a path of stars within the Milky Way that leads to the end of the earth at Finistera.

Whatever the exact origins of the discovery of the tomb of Saint James, over the following 400 years visions of Saint James were reported at every important battle during the Christian re-conquest of Spain culminating in a vision during the decisive battle of Las Navas de Tolosa in 1212. As a result of these visions Saint James became the central figure in the re-Christianisation of Spain and eventually became the patron saint of Spain.

The first documented pilgrimage to Santiago was in 950 and this date is viewed as the start of the Camino. The importance of the Camino of Santiago grew massively from the 10th century and by the 13th century it rivalled both Rome and Jerusalem. To try and understand the importance of the Camino in middle ages, it is worth noting that at its peak Santiago had half a million pilgrims a year when the population of Europe was only 70 million at a time when most people never left the village they were born in. In modern day terms this would represent over five million pilgrims per year compared to the 300 000 pilgrims a year who currently make a pilgrimage to Santiago. During the middle ages, the trade pilgrimage generated made Santiago one of the wealthiest and finest cities in the world. The reformation started a gradual but profound decline in pilgrims. But it was the hiding of and subsequent loss of the remains of St. James in 1589 from a feared invasion by Sir Francis Drake that put the Camino in abeyance for more than three centuries.

The rebirth of interest in the Camino has been attributed to many factors including the decline of formal worship in Spain but for this author and for many others the introduction to the Way of Saint James had its foundation in the Brazilian author, Paulo Coelho's 1987 spiritual novel "O Diário de Um Mago" ("The Pilgrimage"). As can be seen from the statistics the Camino has gained growing popularity since the early 1990s. This has been further fuelled in the English-speaking world by Emilio Estevez's inspirational 2011 film "The Way". Whatever reason causes you to take that first step on the Way of Saint James, this author prays that you too experience the same wonder and the beauty that he experienced on his first Camino.

Finally, I really hope this guidebook has been of help to you in making your Camino. If there is anything you would like to change or add to this guide to improve it for future pilgrims, please let me know by email at mm3guides@gmail.com .

Buen Camino!
Mark McCarthy,
May 30th, 2015.
Updated December 29th, 2017.

Made in the USA
Lexington, KY
10 June 2018